"2000"

Millie Walker

from

Marilyn Magolin

W9-CED-212

It's About Home

CREATING A PLACE TO CHERISH

Patsy Clairmont

JANET KOBOBEL GRANT, EDITOR

VINE BOOKS

SERVANT PUBLICATIONS, ANN ARBOR, MICHIGAN

© 1998 by Patsy Clairmont
All rights reserved.

Vine Books is an imprint of Servant Publications especially designed to serve evangelical Christians.

Unless otherwise noted, Scripture quotations are from The Holy Bible, New International Version (NIV) © 1973, 1984 by International Bible Society, used by permission of Zondervan Publishing House. Other Scripture quotations are from: the New King James Version (NKJV) © 1984 by Thomas Nelson, Inc.; the King James Version (KJV); New American Standard Bible (NASB) © 1960, 1977 by the Lockman Foundation.

Published by Servant Publications
P.O. Box 8617
Ann Arbor, Michigan 48107

Editor: Janet Kobobel Grant
Photography: Bob Foran, Ann Arbor, Michigan

99 00 01 10 9 8 7 6 5 4 3

ISBN 1-56955-101-4

CIP Data on file with the Library of Congress.
Printed in Mexico

In celebration and in memory of

Lena Clairmont,

my dear mother-in-law,

who devoted her life

to cherishing her family.

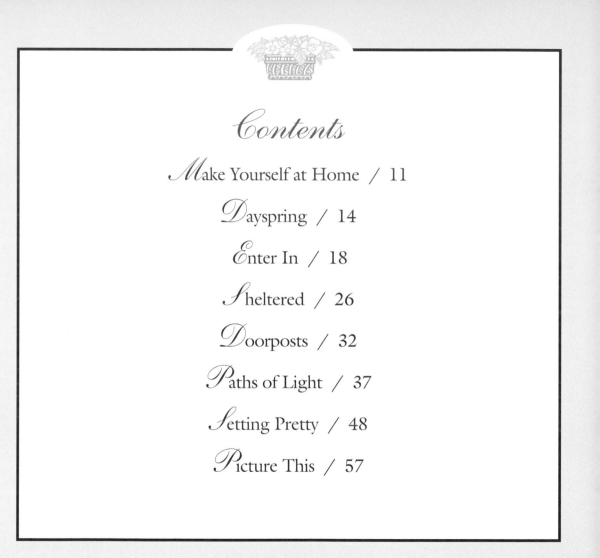

Contents

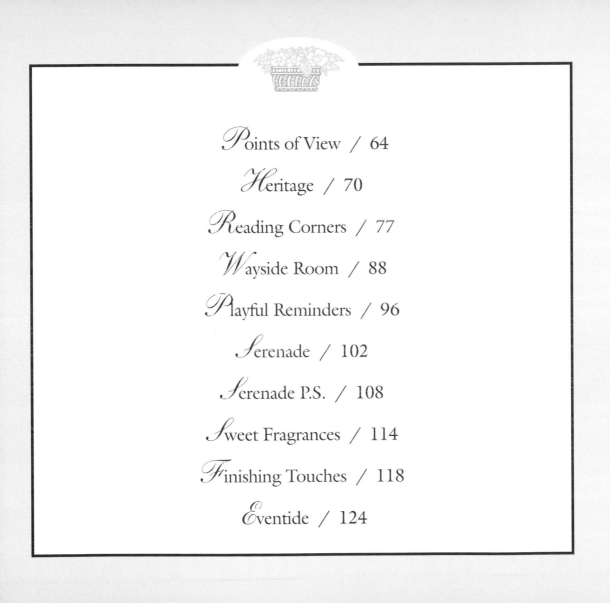

Acknowledgements

*M*any thanks to those who were so helpful in this home project. To my great relief my family and friends rallied to assist me with last minute photographic details. Their all-out efforts made the dreaded word "deadline" feel more like "lifeline," as they extended themselves in supportive and creative ways. Their generosity blessed me and enhanced *It's About Home*.

Any book I have written to date has been expedited by my husband Les' willingness to help make space in my schedule for writing time. Thanks, Honey, for keeping the grill lit, the phone covered, and for hanging up your own clothes. Also for your insightful suggestions along the way. (If you notice Les' absence in the pictures, he's really not camera-shy; he was ill during the photo days and was unable to join in the fun. He is doing well now.)

My sons, Marty and Jason, and my daughter-in-law Danya, continue to make invaluable contributions in practical, emotional, and relational ways to my life. I am one grateful momma. Thank you.

My gifted friend Ginny Lukei travelled across the nation to be my sidekick during the days of picture-taking (talk about over and beyond the call of duty). She offered and implemented suggestions that added artsy dynamics to our efforts. Thank you for your magic touch and your dear spirit.

My lifelong friend Carol Porter was, as usual, at my side, cheerleading. Thanks, Carol, for years of sweet memories and for your ongoing artistic contributions—you've added color to my life. Your friendship makes me feel right at home.

Many thanks to the following three Brighton area businesses and their owners: "Somewhere in Time" store owner and friend Ann Meredith whose good taste and merry heart are a gift to my life. "Brighton Stained Glass Store" owners and friends, Dan Szymanski and Randy Howell, whose hallmark is their generosity and humor. And "Colleen's Rose Garden" whose new friendship caused my home to blossom in the dead of winter. Thank you, thank you, thank you.

Always my heart fills with gratitude when I consider my editor and friend Janet Kobobel Grant. The integrity of your work adds strength to my efforts. Thank you for respecting my love for words while continually expanding my world with your plethora of knowledge.

Bert Ghezzi, thank you for your eager response to this project. Your warm heart and your mischievous ways are a delightful mix. The Servant team has been such a joy to work with and has extended to me a true spirit of hospitality from the president, Don Cooper, to the advertising department, the art department, and the editorial staff. Thank you, Diane Bareis, for being so easy to work with and for your exceptional eye.

Different people along my journey have helped me learn how to infuse my home with richness, none more than my mom, Rebecca Ann McEuen. Mom, I could never thank you enough. Thanks also to Edith Gelaude, Margret Zander, Ginny Lukei, and Florence Littauer, for allowing me to be a part of your homes. You taught me more than you realize.

This book is about *home* and as you can see it has taken many people to prepare it for guests. But now we've shaken the rugs, dusted the furniture, and taken out the garbage, so come on in—we've been waiting for you.

$\mathcal{M}$ake Yourself at Home

$\mathcal{C}$ome in! I'm glad you stopped by for a visit. I know life is full and your days demanding, which makes your visit all the sweeter. While you're here, I want to give you a tour of my home. Together we can amble through and talk about what matters in our surroundings and how to create a place to cherish.

For me, cozy corners are a must. I enjoy being enfolded by a friendly chair with pleasurable belongings at my fingertips—items that please my eyes, nurture my mind, and feed my spirit. We'll pause at my miniature galleries, and I'll introduce you to some of my family and friends. We can chat about spiritual life and physical life and how they intersect in our home lives. After all, homes are personal and provisional, nurturing us in ways we aren't always alert to. And we can tell a lot about a person by entering her home. So come along....

I give you permission to peek in my closets (wearing a hard hat might be wise) and to check out my kitchen drawers. If you feel up to it, would you unravel my appliance cords while you're rummaging around?

No, my home is not—nor has it ever been—perfectly ordered. It, instead, is a mix of neatness and disarray. I do not alphabetize my pantry (in fact, I don't have a pantry), but I admire those who do. My canned asparagus has been rubbing shoulders with the pitted olives for some time now without an adverse reaction. I did notice once, though, that when I set the cider vinegar in the cupboard close to the sweet peas the peas tasted a little loopy.

It's About Home is not about getting our act together, but we will consider our environment and the influence it can have on others and ourselves. We'll examine what our homes are whispering (or shouting) to those who enter and how to enhance those statements.

Sometimes we say more than we mean to about ourselves through our homes. My humor can be noted by my garlic keeper— a clay pot with an animated face only another cracked pot could love. And, yes, much to the embarrassment of my grown children, I selected the busy couch in the living room.

Along with our personalities, our family histories also influence our home life. You'll find rubber bands on the doorknobs in my house. That's the way my mom stored them in her homes. She probably did it for convenience; I do it for remembrance. In many ways a home becomes our tangible expression of love and acceptance of those we care for most.

So, as my kinfolk would say, "Take a load off your feet and sit a spell." I'll pour us some tea and then together we'll begin. We'll start by rolling up a shade on a new day, consider a myriad of ways to enhance our homes both physically and spiritually, and close with lights out in eventide as we say good night with prayers and praise.

Please step into the interior of this book and make yourself right at home.

Sunrise stirs a bright horizon,
As morning taps on entry doors.

Windows wide, anticipating
Daylight's dance across wooden floors.

Summer's breath blousing lace curtains,
Garden's balm sown throughout the room.

Rejoicing prayers offered up,
For dayspring's bride and eventide's groom.

Dayspring

The ritual of opening my house to a new day allows me to invite in the wonder of a fresh beginning. It also gives me a visual check on my world—the weather, the garden, the bird feeders, my neighbor's welfare, and the newspaper's arrival. In dayspring's light I amble through my home lifting shades, drawing back curtains, and parting shutters. I feel as if I'm awakening each room, offering it yet another chance to afford cheer, comfort, and refuge to its daytime visitors.

Because my tendency has been to enter into the morning drowsily, I have had to set my mind toward praise. We didn't create day and we can't uncreate day, but we can purpose to join the daylight hours with an uplifted heart. Praise boosts my lagging spirit and causes me to be grateful for the moments allotted to me. Besides, I find it inspiring to take morning by the hand and guide her through my home.

I remember when I was a child, my mom would softly call my name until I awoke or would gently jostle my shoulder until my sleepy eyes would focus. That's how I encourage my home into a day. Instead of calling the rooms by name, I whisper prayers throughout....

"Dear Lord, when individuals enter my home today, I want them to feel a sense of acceptance and safety. May they, even for a brief interval, be uplifted. For life can be worrisome and at times lonely. So whether it is a deliveryman, a family member, or my dearest friend, may all feel welcomed and valued. Amen."

I tossle the rooms into awareness with the fluff of a pillow, the smoothing of a coverlet, and the clearing of the counters. Once I have draped my robe on a closet hook, dressed, and put out fresh linens, I climb the steps to my office. There I nudge myself into focus with morning devotions.

I love the reminder that "joy comes in the morning," for there is something so healing and renewing about daylight's movement upon the land. With deliberate grace the light dispels the darkness, searching into the very corners to illuminate. Even dreary days bring greater light than the night. I personally enjoy cloudy days, especially ones with a chill in the air. Those times lend themselves to deep-cushioned chairs, charming novels, and crackling fireplaces.

What are your morning rituals? Perhaps you first let out the dog, turn on the coffee, or wake up the kids. May I suggest that tomorrow, as you go about your regimen, you consciously invite in the day as you would a friend and breathe out your first grateful prayers.

> Every morning, lean thine arms awhile
> Upon the window sill of heaven,
> And gaze upon the Lord.
> Then, with that vision in thy heart,
> Turn strong to meet the day.
>
> ANONYMOUS

Morning Prayers:

"Lord, may your footsteps fill our homes and may we be wise enough to walk in them. To follow you throughout the day allows us a kinder perspective, a healing touch, and a genuine enthusiasm for others. We invite you, Lord, not just to visit but to reside in our houses. Without you we would be strangers full of conflict and disappointment, but with you we can embrace each other in peace and compassion. Satisfy our needs with your hospitable presence. Amen."

"Lord, fill this living room with your living presence. Stretch out your arms and enfold our visitors as they stop to chat. For some, their day will have been long and their paths strewn with discord. Cause their tensions to ease and their breathing to deepen. When our guests go their way, may they be aware of the prayers that follow them. Amen."

"This day, which is part of your great design, O Lord, ignites our hearts with praise. Like the rising of the sun we lift our hands in celebration of life and breath and you. As our homes come alive in the sunshine, may our hearts be illuminated by your grace-filled, infiltrating love. Please tidy the unkempt corners and dusty sills of our interior beings as we tend to the same within our dwellings. We welcome your presence in our hearts and in our homes. Amen."

Enter In

When my husband, Les, and I travel by car, I often say to him, as houses whip past us, "I wonder what's behind that front door?" Especially when we're in the country and we pass by a farmhouse, I imagine the aroma of fresh-baked pies (custard and blueberry) and the bustling sounds of the homeowners as they prepare for guests. Of course, in my mind, I'm the guest because I want to see what's behind their door (and eat those pies!).

Doors allow us to enter each other's lives. Doors can say "welcome," doors can say "private," and doors can say "stay out." They can be solid in a formidable way, or they can be transparent in a pleasing way. Some doors are curtained while others allow you a preview before you step in. I find double doors impressive, revolving doors inventive, and Dutch doors playful.

Then there are famous doors such as the ones at the octagonal Baptistery of St. John in Florence, Italy. Artisan Lorenzo Ghiberti, a true Renaissance man, carved in high relief two of the most beautiful doors in the world, referred to as the "Gates of Paradise." Ghiberti devoted almost a quarter of a century to work on the twenty-eight-paneled doors. Twenty of the panels depict Christ's life while eight panels portray the four Evangelists and the Fathers of the church (Ghiberti, as was the tradition of the time, added his own likeness). At the end of the artist's life, he said the doors were his finest work. A person would want to linger long as he or she walked through any doors that took twenty-five years to create.

The Georgian architecture of Dublin, Ireland, features brightly painted doors. These eye-pleasers are adorned with handsome hardware, ornate door knockers, and fanlight windows. As an added enhancement, lacy wrought iron railings line the steps leading up to many of the doors. The homes sit nudged together shoulder to shoulder, placing the doorways in proximity to each other. This array of primary-colored doors lights up the streets with a vibrant welcome.

Niece Brenda and her Yorkshire, Rufus, arrive for a visit.

Have you considered that, like those flamboyant Irish doors, your front door is your first greeting to guests? I'd always thought my welcome began when people entered my home, but then I noticed how cheered I felt when I approached a house with a lovely door. It didn't have to be carved or lacquered, just well tended.

That made me pay special attention to the door of our home. Built in the 1920s, our house wears a deep brown coat of paint with contrasting, soft yellow trim. The house sits back from the road about forty-five feet, creating a sense of reserve. Closer to the road, five white pines tower at least seventy-five feet into the air. I find the house's quiet demeanor soul-soothing and want visitors to feel the same.

We have intersecting sidewalks that come from the roadway and the driveway to meet at the porch steps. You access our main door through the porch. The oak door itself has a rectangular, full-length beveled glass that is curtained with sheared lace. This lacy doorway sets the tone for the rest of the house and communicates to visitors our sincere invitation to enter and make themselves at home.

That's how I felt when I was on vacation and happened to spy an older home's handsome door. I marched right up on the porch to investigate more closely. The showy, antique hardware and the oval, leaded-glass window on the door were exquisite. I so wanted to interview the homeowners regarding their door's jewelry, but, alas, no one was home.

My editor and friend, Janet, told me she was asked to tend a neighbor's home while the family was away. The instructions for entering the home were like none Janet had heard before. Get this: The door had no doorknob. Hmm, talk about tricky. The door was always secured from the inside; otherwise someone could accidentally lean against it and the door would pop open. Just call me old-fashioned, but I think I'll stick with the turn-the-doorknob routine.

Another home I visited had a wreath on the door with a note that read, "Please ring doorbell as birds have nested in our wreath and knocking irritates them." That made me giggle. I thought anyone who extended such considerate hospitality to the birds must be great with real-life folks … and she was.

Speaking of doorbells, I love ones that ring loudly enough that you know they work. I find it disconcerting to ring a doorbell, hear no sound, and wonder if I should begin to pound. Besides, a melodic doorbell is a way to add a few pleasant notes to the day.

My friend Carol, owner of a Victorian home, has one of her doors flanked by wooden swans filled with flowers. At Christmas they are especially lovely, overflowing with poinsettias and cozied up to the door, with its oval, beveled-glass inset. I always feel greeted even before Carol answers my ring.

In my family it was common, when you knew company was coming, to be in the doorway waiting and then to go out and meet your guests. I know that isn't always possible, but, when it is, it's so hospitable and makes the entry into your home even more memorable. Knowing you are pleased to receive your guests will warm their hearts.

That open-door policy certainly touched the Prodigal Son. His father even rushed out to embrace him. Imagine how meaningful that must have been for this bedraggled young man. Despite his reckless lifestyle, he was welcomed and loved. That tells me an open door into relationships is even more desirable than the most ornate physical doors you could ever install in your home.

I, too, know how it feels to receive merciful love, because I was a prodigal daughter. I ran away from home when I was sixteen. After a short time, I wanted to go home but feared my parents' reaction to my poor judgment. Finally, dejected, I returned. I can still see Mom in my mind's eye. She ran out the front door, down the driveway, and, with open arms and forgiving tears, embraced me.

I was stunned at this undeserved show of love. It caused me to fill with sorrow for having brought my parents such anguish. I guess I thought after I ran that they would lock the door and throw away the key so I couldn't return. Instead, I learned their heart's door was always open to me. What a sense of security that brought, a security I wanted my own children to one day experience, to know they could always come home.

There is One who desires us to know his undeserved love and his security. He longs to be in an ongoing relationship with us. Scripture tells us he is the one who knocks at the door of our heart, seeking entry. He won't barge in, but if we open our heart's door, he promises to come in and partake of life with us. He offers us acceptance and forgiveness that will transform our view of him and of ourselves. Once again I'm stunned—to think the Lord would enter into our lives and remain, like the perfect guest who you think is coming to visit but has decided, much to your delight, to stay.

Not only will the Lord take up residence in our heart's home, but he will also lead and guide our decisions on which future doors we should enter. When opportunity knocks, it isn't necessarily in our best interest to step through every door. I'm grateful that the Lord offers to direct our steps.

By the way, watching one's step and which door one walks through is a wise choice in my home. Small networks of halls ramble willy-nilly through my upstairs. My guests seem to enjoy peeking through each door to see what's there. One of our doors holds a jolting surprise. The door is attractive, even inviting, but when you open it you see that it drops straight down—sans stairs—to the first floor. It is

the door that leads nowhere—unless you are in a hurry for breakfast and don't mind sky diving to retrieve it. I have a brick doorstop positioned snugly against it to prevent children and spontaneous adults from entering in where angels fear to tread.

I, for one, am a spontaneous adult and have been known to vault before I view the possible consequences. So it has been of great value to me to seek and to find the Lord's door-opening counsel. It sure has cut down on my free falls.

My favorite doors at our house are the leaded-glass pair that separate the living room from the dining room. They feature crests in the center that are repeated in a pair of windows in the living room. My rooms are cozy, yet these doors give me a, well, rather a royal feeling. I also appreciate the conversational privacy the doors add while still allowing me visibility. (I don't want to miss anything!)

In the Old Testament the Levites were selected by the Lord to care for the Tabernacle, which included the entries. Four thousand men were assigned to maintain and guard the doors (gates). Obviously, being a keeper of the doors—whether for the Tabernacle or for a home—is an honored position. The psalmist tells us, "I would rather be a doorkeeper in the house of my God than dwell in the tents of the wicked" (Psalm 84:10b).

Doors are important: they allow or deny entry. They are a tangible and necessary boundary. Walk around your home and check out your doors. What does your front door say to your guests? How about all the other doors in your home? In what ways can you convey "welcome" or "private" or "don't take life so seriously" through your doors?

Perhaps we should proclaim a National Door Day to spruce up and secure our doors. And, more important, we should have a worldwide Spiritual Door Day in which we listen for the Lord's knock. Can you picture that? People of all nations leaning to hear him. Think how thrilling if, in response to the Lord's tap, tap, tapping, we threw open our doors and leaped into his waiting arms.

$\mathscr{S}$heltered

$\mathscr{I}$ love a porch that encircles a home like a warm hug. I love open porches that suggest availability, especially ones lined with inviting chairs that wordlessly recruit passersby to sit a spell and catch their breaths. I love tiny porches that promise intimate chats and friendly secrets and expansive porches that insist on peopled celebrations. I appreciate porches that beckon me out of the storm and into their safe covering. And ones so grand that people snap endless pictures from their cars as they cruise by.

I am a hopeless romantic when it comes to porches. I think every home should have at least one. Perhaps I long for bygone times when neighbors called from their porches to yours to see how your day fared. When even strangers were greeted as they sauntered by, and children were given peppermints as they jump-roped past your porch. When schedules weren't so hectic, leaving time for carefree chats and leisurely spells of rocking.

And don't forget the swing, oh, please don't forget the porch swing. Days become swirls of lovely colors in the sway of a porch swing. The creaking becomes a sweet melody that allows one to ruminate rhythmically. And everyone knows a proper porch swing comes arrayed with pillows for those delicious moments when one

successfully rocks oneself to sleep. The swing is the porch's poetry.

I have to confess that at the moment I am swingless (talk about deprivation). My family and I rocked the last one into oblivion. In fact, Les, our son Jason, and I were having a Sunday swing on our open porch on a former home when suddenly the anchored bolts cast anchor and deposited us in triplicate. Now that was startling. I therefore recommend a routine check on your hardware. (Hindsight, no pun intended, is always 20/20.) Since we have not yet replaced our swing, we fill our swing needs with a glider and an array of rockers. (Note that it takes several items to stand in for one porch swing.) I guess we never outgrow our need to be cradled, which is probably why we all love hugs, rockers, and swings.

In the romantic movie *Somewhere in Time*, many of the scenes take place on and in front of the Grand Hotel's porch on Mackinac Island in my home state of Michigan. I've only been to the island twice, but both times I made sure I took time to eye the famous long porch. Because so many visitors are drawn to the hotel and particularly the porch, a foot toll is charged for any nonguests perusing it. Seems we spectators were nudging out the paying guests who desired to dream away a portion of their day viewing the beautiful grounds from the comfort of the Grand's verandah. I don't blame them. When my ship (or rowboat) comes in, I'm going to moor it in the Mackinac Island Harbor in Lake Huron, strut into the hotel, sign in, and take up my viewing spot in the shade. Occasionally, I'll wave to the passersby.

Until then, I'm thoroughly enjoying my own porch. Petite and enclosed, it perches at the top of our front steps. Because of its position, the porch offers extended visibility up and down North Second Street. I have filled our little shelter with an antique wicker table and chairs in hopes of sharing a cozy cup of tea and a saucerful of secrets with a friend or two. I have also included an old, carved rocker with throw; a Victorian table and lamp; a small fountain; and a profuse bouquet of morning glories. Friends and family seem to enjoy just passing through the tiny porch, and deliverymen seem grateful to take refuge in it out of our unpredictable weather. If I'm not home when a

delivery is attempted, I'm thankful for dry packages safely nestled inside my porch when I return.

We also have a back, enclosed porch that one might refer to as "abbreviated." Truth is, if I held my breath, Les and I might both fit in it at the same time. It's about the size of a telephone booth, but even so it's personable and functional. It allows one to wipe off her feet and have a moment of reprieve from rain or snow while prying off the keys that have frozen to her gloves (I love winter).

To enter this porchette, you must climb a few steps and walk across a deck. Our dream is to transform the deck into a covered, if not enclosed, porch. (Enclosed porches, while not being as openly hospitable, are more useful in the Midwest, with its frequent blasts of inclement weather.) We would then have layered porches.

I doubt if that look will catch on.

My husband's home territory, the Upper Peninsula of Michigan, boasts many homes with the layered look. They sport a covered porch and a small inner porch called a shed. The shed allows one to stamp off some of the 240 inches of seasonal snowfall and to grab an armload of dry wood to help keep the home fires burning.

Yes, a porch is a good thing. How about yours? Is it all set to offer an array of services to you and yours? It can be a place to receive guests and packages. A place to sip tea and visit. A grand place to take meals, park boots, sneak naps, read books, work puzzles, write letters, and watch for guests. But my favorite porch feature is that of a visible sign of refuge and shelter.

Scripture says the Lord God is a refuge and a shelter to those seeking safety. "How priceless is your unfailing love! Both high and low among men find refuge in the shadow of your wings" (Psalm 36:7). During inclement times we can go to him, and he allows us to slip under his wings. Trust me, this is even better than a porch swing!

But how does one find the comfort and protection of the Lord?

First, "Be still, and know that I am God" (Psalm 46:10a).

When I stop whatever I'm doing (working, worrying, whining) and become still, I realize the Lord is with me—not always because I can feel his presence, but because he has promised it. "I will never leave you nor forsake you" (Hebrews 13:5b, NKJV).

Second, "I will remember the deeds of the Lord; yes, I will remember your miracles of long ago" (Psalm 77:11).

My personal history with the Lord is a dear reminder and a comforting agent in my life. When I think back on his lovingkindness, my pulse begins to beat more evenly. Also, the ways that he secured his people in the Bible help to anchor my sometimes wavering heart. Recalling your history and the history of God's people can calm your unsettled mind.

Third, "Ask and it will be given to you; seek and you will find; knock and the door will be opened to you" (Matthew 7:7).

Ask God in some tangible way to show you his protective covering and then take note. He may do that through the Scriptures (yes, they are concrete), through a messenger, through a dream, through your thoughts, through nature, through … well, there is no end to his creative methods of communication.

Fourth, "My people will live in peaceful dwelling places, in secure homes, in undisturbed places of rest" (Isaiah 32:18).

Purpose to go to the Lord for shelter, and then don't leave your resting place. No, we can't stay on the porch, but when we must leave our physical shelter we can take our spiritual shelter, the Lord, with us in our hearts and minds. What a relief. What security. What a shelter.

Doorposts

*D*oorposts are the two side pieces of a doorframe—that holds the door in place, the support system for our entries and exits. They are something we hardly take note of, and yet without them our doors would not stay solidly in place. Our security, therefore, would be jeopardized, leaving us vulnerable to thieves, weather, and unwanted guests (scoundrels).

I don't know about you, but I don't think much about foundational things in a home … until they are threatened. When Les and I looked at homes on the market we each had our territory. While I was looking at the layout of the house, he was checking out the ceilings for roof leaks. While I was counting the sinks in the bathroom, he was examining the plumbing. As I oohed and aahed over the fireplace, Les scrutinized the chimney's construction. Les is a foundational man, and I am a blueprint woman. But how long would my blueprint plan stand without a strong foundation? Thank the Lord for Les.

In the book of Deuteronomy, the Lord instructs his people on how to have foundational faith (6:6-9). He encourages them to press his commandments into their own hearts while instilling them into their children. He said his ways should be a regular part of their conversations wherever their day might lead them. The Lord then takes his point a step further when he says they should wear his words on their hands and their foreheads. And then he concludes this list by instructing them to write his commands on both the doorposts and the gates.

That's pretty all-encompassing and reminds us of the foundational importance of carrying his words with us wherever we go. I'm not talking about toting a two-ton Bible with which to wow and whack others. We don't want ruptures but righteousness. That comes as we study, memorize, learn, and walk in his ways. Then, at every turn his word is influencing us, protecting us, and affecting others.

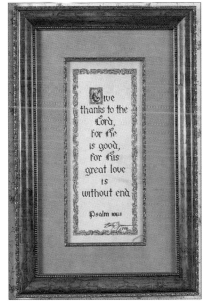

I like to display Scripture in my home. It becomes for me a daily reminder, a gentle accountability, and a foundational offering I quietly can extend to others. I don't have it on my doorposts, but I do have it in my living room, dining room, and office.

On my office wall hangs a compelling picture of a lamb in softly falling snow. The subdued coloring, the lamb's tenderness, and the delicate snowflakes cause one to stop and ponder this print. Tucked below the little lamb in small script are these powerful words, "Redeemed … with the precious blood of Christ, as of a lamb without blemish and without spot" (1 Peter 1:18–19, KJV).

In both my living room and dining room I have Scriptures in flourishing calligraphy. The familiar and foundational statement from Joshua is in our living room: "Choose you this day whom ye will serve; … but as for me and my house, we will serve the Lord" (Joshua 24:15b, KJV). Then a dear reminder from the Psalms hangs in our old-fashioned dining room: "Give thanks to the Lord, for he is good; his love endures forever" (Psalm 106:1).

In my hallway is a picture (no verse) of Christ in Gethsemane pleading in prayer. You've probably seen it any number of times; it is an old, popular print. This particular one hung in my grandmother's home and then my mother's. Even without words it speaks volumes to the heart of scriptural truth.

When I was nine, my mom invited Christ to rule her heart and permeate her home. One of the ways I was aware of his loving invasion was a Bible that became a visible reality in our house of the Lord's invisible work in my mom's life. The Bible was black leather and of generous size and weight. A gold sketch of the Lord as the Good Shepherd tending some sheep was rendered on the front cover. It was a King James, red-letter edition with a thumb index. Lovely pictures appeared throughout, with one section on the Sermon on the Mount artistically featured. I haven't seen that Bible in years, yet I remember it vividly. What golden memories that image stirs of a mom who stayed close to her Shepherd like a lamb as she searched out his Word.

My grandmother, even into her nineties, would sit at her dining room table with her extra-large-print Bible open and her magnifying glass held at an angle for her bifocaled, cataract-clouded eyes to catch each word. She would whisper it aloud as she read and then faithfully fill in the answers in her Sunday school lesson book. Her Bible wasn't leather, but it had the same weathered look as my mom's because these two women turned to foundational truth to make it through life. To see the Good Book lying on a table or resting on the arm of a chair in both my mother's and grandmother's homes was to grow up with a sense of Scripture as an integral part of life.

Have you made room in your decorating scheme for the Scriptures? Today artists have created attractive, even breathtaking, renderings of the Bible's truths. Even refrigerator magnets are available with verse inscriptions. Ladies, what do we frequent any more, uh, frequently than the food bins? Or you may be artistic yourself and choose to needlepoint, paint, or letter your favorite verses or stories to display in your home.

In deciding what verse to use, you might want to consider your life verse. This is a verse or passage you feel (under the direction of the Holy

Spirit's leading) is what you want the Lord to teach you deeply. One that you pray regularly, that you memorize, and to the best of your ability that you live out daily. In other words, it's one that is written on the spiritual doorposts (the framework) of your life.

My life verse is Psalm 1:1-3, with the emphasis on verse 3.

¹"How blessed is the man who does not walk in the counsel of the wicked, nor stand in the path of sinners, nor sit in the seat of scoffers!

²"But his delight is in the law of the Lord, and in His law he meditates day and night.

³"And he will be like a tree firmly planted by streams of water, which yields its fruit in its season, and its leaf does not wither; and in whatever he does, he prospers" (NASB).

Yes, this bush-height, blueprint woman wants to grow into a splendid tree with deep, foundational roots. I want my life and therefore my home to offer refuge, shade, and fruit. I have come to recognize that growth is a lifelong process. The Lord is looking for progress, not perfection, and I am grateful.

Okay, now it's your turn. What's your verse? If you don't have one, today is a good day to ask God's Spirit to imprint one on your doorposts. The Scriptures will help you establish a firm foundation that will carry you through the years.

$\mathcal{P}$aths of Light

$\mathcal{M}$y husband loves ceiling lights: with one flick of a switch he floods every corner with visual clarity. I, however, prefer soft pools of lamplight. I appreciate the warm guidance they offer from one side of the room to the other, from one lamp to another. So Les and I have conceded to each other and our home now offers both types of light. Depending on what evening you visit and who is there to greet and seat you, you will either be blinded by floodlights or find yourself stumbling to a chair. Actually we've put dials on our overheads to modulate Les' light and we've added to my lamp collection to illuminate your path. Teamwork in action.

A number of years ago I visited my Memphis friend Nancy Stephenson; that is when my passion for lamps deepened. Nancy's handsome home, filled with her unique and artistic touches, is truly an experience to be remembered. I have had the good fortune of being her houseguest on a number of occasions and have many pleasant memories. One of the highlights for me was observing her evening walk through her home, turning out her lamps. She has them everywhere, but because they are thoughtfully placed you don't seem to notice how many there are until it's time to retire and she makes her rounds.

Son Jason and daughter-in-law, Danya, help to keep the home lights burning.

I loved how each lamp had its own illuminating form. Some of the lamps spilled most of their light out the bottom of their shades as if purposing to expose a particular chair beneath it or feature a lovely bouquet or book on the table below. (Have you noticed how lamplight both displays and plays with the wood of a table? It showcases the spectacular grain, while on the edge of its circle of illumination the lamp's light playfully mixes with the shadows, creating little creatures of the night.)

Other lamps broadcasted much of their offering out the top of the shade, brightening a wall sconce or directing one to necessary switches. Some lamps stood tall and offered choices of lighting intensity while others were candlelike. I found myself warmed by her lamps, which invited me to converse, read, and rest. I also enjoyed the softly lit path that guided me to the guest room. It too was illuminated by an array of small lamps, which I found hospitable and comforting.

Nancy's lamps, like my own today, are eclectic. That's a fun way to say they come in varying sizes and shapes and were purchased over a period of years and in all conditions. We bought them in off-the-road shops, antique stores, and secondhand emporiums. Nancy rewired and redesigned many of hers. She has such an eye for style, shape, and salvageability that she rescues true treasures that most of us would initially overlook and later, after her transforming touch, desire.

When Nancy visited my home, we were living in a church camp setting. It was very different from her stately home … believe me. Nancy was a gracious guest. One  evening a sudden storm blew out all the lights in our hilltop house. I took an oil lamp to my wide-eyed guest, who seemed encouraged to have a little light amidst the storm. I couldn't resist snapping a picture of her holding that lamp in her long nightgown, appearing as if she had just stepped out of a Miss Marple mystery. Later, when I developed my pictures, I thought how appropriate to capture her in flickering light, for Nancy will always be my lamplighter friend, the one who exposed me to the beauty of a softly lit home.

Several of the lamps that softly light my home belonged to my mom. Mom loved globed lamps, especially antique ones, and collected a number of them throughout the years. Many moves and many years have whittled down Mom's collection to a precious few. One of my favorites is a Banquet lamp. It is tall and delicately ornate, and the hand painted floral globe casts a warm glow. What I appreciate most, though, is not its age but the fact that it was my mom's and graced her home. Mom taught me by example to appreciate and care for lovely things. How pleased I am that I can now care for items she once looked after. Somehow that helps me feel closer to her (she lives in Florida), and it gives me a sense of watching over some of our family's physical history.

A number of years ago my mom came to visit with a tiny treasure tucked under her arm. She had stopped with some friends at a garage sale and purchased a darling lamp for me. The lamp base is a young woman—perhaps a shepherdess or a peasant girl—leaning against a fence. She's quite sweet and, even though the shade is weathered, its ecru aging seems appropriate. So I haven't replaced it … yet. (I love pre-rogative.)

My husband, he who pooh-poohed my lamps, now makes lamps. Beautiful lamps. Isn't that poetic justice? We have discovered that Les has a natural ability with stained glass. He lays down a pattern, carefully cuts the glass pieces out, then, one by one, solders them. My favorite is a floor lamp we display—actually, I show off in our living room. It is a water lily design with 466 pieces that is both pleasing to the eye and enhancing to our room.

One ceiling light I am fond of is our dining room chandelier. Not only is it on a dial that allows me to soften or brighten its effect, but also it's sized well for the room. Another plus for me is the glistening prisms … until they need to be shined. When we moved into our home the chandelier was hung very close to the ceiling, which gave great visibility of the far wall. But we decided to sacrifice that view for a better look at the light fixture itself. Once we lowered it, it was even prettier than we had realized. In fact, one day the former owner stopped by to pick up some mail and was smitten with our lovely chandelier and wondered where we had purchased it.

When I told her it was the one she had left behind she was surprised. She had looked at it for years from the bottom up, but from eye level it had a whole new appearance.

Several ceiling fixtures appear to be original to our house. They are quite attractive but small and use low-wattage lightbulbs, which means they give less light than a lamp. This is disturbing to Light-Man Les, but because we believe they are original we both hesitate to remove them. So we have had to sprinkle in more lamps (which hasn't hurt my feelings). This has given me an excuse to playfully add a myriad of, shall we say, light touches.

Along with my passion for lamps of varied descriptions nestled throughout my home, including a white rabbit lamp burrowed in the living room, I'm also an avid candle collector. I think overhead lights are like shouts while candles are whispers. Whether they are short, spiraled, tapered, pudgy, or electric—whatever their dimensions—I'm a fan. I feel candles send a variety of messages: they intimate "we've been waiting for you," they quietly insist on celebrations, they flicker romantic notions, and they burn as a witness of hope. Have you noticed that when someone lights candles at a dinner or for a guest's visit, the occasion takes on added significance? It says "this time together is important." The whisper of the candlelight becomes a resounding shout in our hearts that we are special. The stipulation, though, at my house is that my candles may not be (achoo!) fragranced.

In addition to candles I also appreciate fireplaces. Even though the fireplace can be sooty and the logs can be, uh, loggie, when they are ablaze I feel snuggly. A dancing fireplace adds to the intrigue of a book, thaws icy mittens, cheers guests, or even melts a cold heart. During Michigan blizzards, losing electricity isn't unusual; that's when our fireplaces crackle with renewed purpose, providing both warmth and light.

Despite my passion for lamplight, I love a dark room for sleeping. My light-loving husband appreciates an illuminated path in the night for practical purposes and safety, so on his side of the bed near the floor is a night-light pointing him in the right direction while additional light sources in the hall help him find his way.

The exception to my dark-room preference is when I'm ill. Then I prefer a gentle lamplight to be aglow in my room. I find waking up in pain in the dark disconcerting, if not frightening, whereas when I wake up in lamplight I can more easily gain my

bearings. I find soft light to be reassuring, especially during dark hours.

In the 1850s dark hours cast deadly shadows in British hospitals as soldiers in the Crimean War died by the scores. Their deaths were caused not by the wounds they incurred in battle but by diseases they contracted convalescing in the hospital. The British government turned to Florence Nightingale to help, and she and her thirty-eight-woman nursing staff did an astounding thing. They brought the hospital death rate down from a shocking 42 percent to a miraculous 2 percent with Florence's stringent rules of cleanliness for her staff and her patients.

Florence, who was born to a wealthy family, decided against her family's wishes to become a nurse. In those times nursing was considered one of the lowest and dreariest of occupations. But Florence believed that God had instructed her to light her lamp and carry healing to those in physical agony.

Florence not only saved many lives during those war-torn years, but she also changed the nursing profession forever. After the war Florence founded a nursing school and was the inspiration for the founding of the Red Cross. She became known as the Lady with the Lamp for she brought the light of change, the light of compassion, and the light of cleanliness to the dark hours of human suffering. She provided a path of light to a new way of caring for others.

Our Christmas luminaria remind me of how helpful, encouraging, and necessary a lit path can be. Some years ago Les and I hosted a holiday dinner at a church camp. We realized the guests would have trouble finding their way to the celebration if we didn't somehow illuminate the path in our dark country setting. So Les cut out wooden trumpeting angels, put them on twenty-four-inch dowels, stuck the dowels in the ground, and placed luminaria on the ground beneath them. Many people expressed not only their appreciation for the guidance but also how pleased they were to have a band of angels trumpeting their arrival.

Speaking of arrivals, one day, one grand day, at the sound of an angel's trumpet, Jesus who is the Light of the World will arrive for his children. We will then be with him forever and ever and ever. And guess what? No need for night-lights, flashlights, or traffic lights. There will be no chandeliers, fireplaces, floodlights, or porch lights. Street lights will be obsolete, candles will finally flicker out, and lamplight will be permanently snuffed. For Jesus will be our Infinity Illuminator. Alleluia!

Until then we (little limited illuminators) get to hold down the fort, keep the home fires burning, tend to the oil in our lamps, and be extensions of his brilliance. Now is our opportunity to be Ladies with the Lamps carrying hope to a sooty world. That's the glorious thing about light—it makes a difference. So let's keep our wicks trimmed and our jars filled with oil.

An ongoing source of oil for my lamp are the Scriptures, which are filled with light-giving counsel. The Word is often a floodlight searching into the corners of my heart. It fuels the passion of my faith. It's the wick that allows the light of Christ to be seen in my life. It steadies my faith and adds to my hope, as I wait on tiptoes for the skies to split open, the trumpets to shout, and heaven's light to immerse the earth.

"Arise, shine, for your light has come, and the glory of the Lord rises upon you. See, darkness covers the earth and thick darkness is over the peoples, but the Lord rises upon you and his glory appears over you. Nations will come to your light, and kings to the brightness of your dawn" (Isaiah 60:1-3).

"You are the light of the world. A city on a hill cannot be hidden. Neither do people light a lamp and put it under a bowl. Instead they put it on its stand, and it gives light to everyone in the house. In the same way, let your light shine before men, that they may see your good deeds and praise your Father in heaven" (Matthew 5:14-16).

"For God, who said, 'Let light shine out of darkness,' made his light shine in our hearts to give us the light of the knowledge of the glory of God in the face of Christ" (2 Corinthians 4:6).

"God is light; in him there is no darkness at all" (1 John 1:5b).

Setting Pretty

Some years ago, eighteen in fact, I was a guest for the first time in Fred and Florence Littauer's home. With their colorful personalities and hospitable spirits, they make a visit a lasting memory.

Each morning, to signal breakfast time, Fred would ring chimes and sing an uplifting song in his deep, rich voice. His song would fill the home's hallways, and we guests would respond by making our way to the front of the house. It was such a pleasant experience to be greeted so joyfully and then to find a festive display awaiting us in the dining room.

The presentation of the table was transformed from meal to meal with different place mats or tablecloths, centerpieces, cloth napkins, napkin rings, and a varied menu. (It was my first experience of eating salsa with my morning eggs. Yum!) The versatile table settings and delectable offerings caused us eagerly to anticipate each mealtime.

Along with their beautiful tables and scrumptious food, the Littauers made us feel welcome with their guided conversations. All the guests were invited to share for a few minutes about their lives. This enabled everyone around the table to be a verbal participant rather than allow a chatty few to monopolize the visit and leave out the

Son Marty hesitates to try Mom's latest recipe. History has proven him wise.

more reserved personalities. By the time the meal was completed, you felt less like a visitor and more like family.

I was amazed to learn that, company or not, Fred and Florence's tables always sported cheerful greetings. Even on an ordinary day, they created an exceptional environment. I guess I had always considered gussied-up tables as preparation for holidays and Sunday company. After experiencing several mornings of the Littauers' breakfast celebrations, I promised myself that I, too, would take the time to design lovely tables for my family, especially on ordinary days. Since then my interest in establishing personality and pizzazz on a tabletop has continued to grow.

When I fancy up a meal with colorful surroundings, my expressive daughter-in-law's face lights up. I've loved raising boys, but I must admit they don't tend to express glee and delight over girlie stuff such as a new set of napkin rings. I do believe, though, that my guys have enjoyed eating at an attractive table. For the record, I am much better at decorating than I am at cooking. For some meals we would have been better off eating the decorations. So, if you drop by, you may want to bring a sack lunch as plan B.

One Fourth of July, we had a barbecue and invited our grown children to join us for hot dogs and steaks. While Les was busy grilling, I was busy creating a gala tabletop. I wanted my table to explode with color so I started with a navy tablecloth and used red and blue bandanna handkerchiefs as napkins with white dishes. (I often use white dishes, which allow me to choose any other color and any theme. They also cheerfully show off accessories.) I flared napkins, one of each color, out of each white ceramic stemmed goblet around the table. To add a touch more color, I placed cobalt-blue luncheon plates on the white dinner plates. At each place were red nut cups filled with white mints, and a small American flag waved from the center of each cup. I arranged a bouquet of red roses in the center of the table and lit white candles just as my guests arrived. Then I waited for daughter-in-law Danya's squeals. I think her favorite part of the decorations was the setting I made for their dog, Pumpkin. I placed her white water bowl, with a small flag affixed to the side of it, in the center of navy and white napkins on the kitchen floor.

I didn't have to work hard or invest a ton of money to make a big statement. The most expensive item ordinarily would be the roses; however, I had received these from a friend a few days before. My white dishes are the same age as Methuselah, but they continue to work well for me. The cobalt dishes were an affordable purchase ($1.50 each) from a discount store and really jazzed up the table. The napkins (hand-kerchiefs) were $1.25 each.

I have often found that the most satisfying touches are things I already have in my home or yard (pine cones, flowers, leaves, branches, boughs). I have a drawerful of goodies I've collected and received from friends over the years. Since writing a tea book, I now have many charming teapot napkin rings that have been sent my way. But for some reason teapots and guys aren't always compatible, so usually I save those for the "girls" (for teatime, luncheons, or birthdays).

Before moving to our current home, Les and I invited our friends, the Bells, for a summer outdoor dinner. Blue and white striped sheets served as our floor-length tablecloths, and I set the table under the pines in our backyard. I used Italian blue and white patterned dishes interspersed with cobalt accessories. Navy napkins with

Table setting includes candleholder used as a butter dish, sporting a bird atop a nest. Note watercolor place cards designed by Carol Porter and hand-loomed rug woven by my sister-in-law Diane Kesanen, used as a runner.

white, ceramic napkin rings were perched in front of the plates like bluebirds waiting for crumbs. A fresh bouquet of black-eyed Susans from my garden added a mirthful splash to the table. Neighbors oohed and aahed over the fences and suggested they should be added to future guest lists.

Perhaps you're thinking, "But I'm just not creative that way." I say, "Be a copycat." That's how I started to spruce up our meal, as I used the Littauers' table as my pattern. Also, many books are available that display lovely settings for mealtime to inspire us.

Through the years Les and I have lived in mini-dwellings, and I have often shied away from group entertaining. We did more one-couple-at-a-time visits. But I have since learned that smaller spaces are underrated. You are far more likely to interact with folks when they are attached to your elbows. Also, when the room is full of folks, a well-prepared small environment can feel more familylike, more nurturing, and more conversational. So I say hurrah for cozy structures. Bring on the crowds—and the creative use of tiny locales.

Our former home was a bit brief in floor space so I had to be creative to accommodate forty guests at a bridal shower for our then future daughter-in-law, Danya. I made more room by stationing my friend Carol on the porch as a greeting hostess with a water jar full of raspberry lemonade. Another friend stood at the door so that, as the guests received their drinks, she could take their gifts. The gifts were then placed on the stairwell leading up to the second floor. That gave the guests room to maneuver their way to the chairs. Our small living room was open to our tiny kitchen as was our dining room. So I put the dining room table in the office, which was off the dining room. That allowed me to set up chairs theater-style in the dining room and living room facing the kitchen. Carol and I used lace curtains to transform a kitchen stool into a princess' throne for Danya and placed it in the kitchen at a small island (draped in a crocheted tablecloth) in view of all the guests for the unwrapping of the gifts. Next to where Danya sat I floated a fragrant gardenia in an old crystal bowl with a lovely candle in a holder positioned nearby. At the close of the shower, I presented Danya's mom with the candle set to thank her for sharing her daughter (the light of her life) with our family.

The food was displayed around the perimeter of the office on antique dishes. Cut-glass cake stands presented the cheesecakes in regal style. An ultra-thin, two-foot vase featured three tall white lilies, making an elegant statement while taking up very little table space. My friend Ann loaned me charming patterned luncheon sets that the

Friends Carol and Ginny join me for brunch.

women placed in their laps as they partook of goodies.

Because we had a plan, our abbreviated space seemed more generous than it was. For that special occasion our little house handled a big memory. Yes, there's a lot to be said for small homes.

Since I've lived in Michigan my entire life, I love autumn hues. So when the winds start to chill and the burning bush shrubbery flames red, I pull out our fruit-patterned dishes along with fall accessories in deep greens, rich rusts, and golden yellows. Those dishes take us through Thanksgiving; then I go back to my white-dish faithfuls that showcase so well the Christmas traditional greens and reds.

For Christmas Eve dinner as well as other times I enjoy using place cards and individual candles at each person's plate. (There's nothing like seeing one's name up in lights.) If you don't want to invest in place card holders, pine cones work fine. Also, oil lamps are a festive plus and speak of warmth in the midst of frosty weather.

Winter settles in for a lengthy stay in the Midwest from November to April, and I find certain colors lift my spirits when the season begins to drag around February. Bright yellows, spring greens, and soft aquas put a twinkle in a gray day. Also, fresh flower bouquets breathe life back into the atmosphere and seem worth the small financial investment for the big emotional dividends. A vibrant bowl of fruit seems to promise warmer days full of sweet produce. And stemmed goblets, whether they are filled with cranberry juice or ice water, please my senses. Add a twist of lemon and a sprig of mint and give me a seed catalogue to leaf through, and I can make it another six weeks until spring can speak for itself.

Food, a necessary and constant part of our lives, is often at the center of our socializing. Partaking of food with others is a personal experience. Have you noticed when you're angry with someone how difficult it is to eat with that person? Often we would rather go without food than share our table with someone who has offended us. And how many times have you lost your appetite over words that were said?

The Lord extends a personal invitation to dine with him. He says, "Here I am! I stand at the door and knock. If anyone hears my voice and opens the door, I will come in and eat with him, and he with me" (Revelation 3:20).

What a divine dining opportunity. Picture this: Your dining room ablaze with candles, your china glistening, goblets filled with fine wine, and he who poured out his life as an offering for you, Jesus, sitting at your table.

He smiled when you opened the door for him because it pleased the Lord that you heard and responded. You took his hand, he squeezed yours, and you thought your heart would burst with love. When you were seated across from him, you realized the food you had prepared was unnecessary, as Jesus' presence had filled you. Dining took on new significance while you spent time with him for those intimate moments with Christ satisfied you in a way no physical meal ever could.

Isn't it puzzling that we so often settle for less? That's not to suggest we give up joyous dining experiences with others, but it serves as a reminder that we not forget Jesus, who longs for times alone with us. When we meet with him, we are far better prepared to then meet with others and serve them creatively. *Bon appétit!*

$\mathscr{P}$icture This

$\mathscr{M}$ay we never grow weary of appreciating or applauding beauty. I see how the Lord sculpted the mountains, watercolored the heavens, molded the terrain, and carved out craters. As if that were not enough, he then tended to the details: He whittled palm trees, spun tulips, and tatted Queen Anne's lace. These and a myriad other creative touches remind me of his love for art.

When the Lord God finished designing the world, he created us and said, "I have made you in my own likeness" (Genesis 1:26). No wonder we have so many creative urges. And how wonderful that we can incorporate beauty in our homes in the form of art and teach our families to appreciate it as well (which, by the way, is sometimes a slow process).

I love art. My reservoir of art knowledge is small, but my desire to learn is great. I can spot certain artists' works from a distance, but only those that are quite well known. My investigation of art has started late in life, and, with the art field so broad, at times I'm a little overwhelmed. I tell you this so others like myself will take heart and press on.

I own a couple of original art pieces because they were done by my great friend and artist Carol Porter. One of my Porter prints is a winter scene of cardinals done

in colored pencil. It greets my guests in the entry. I commissioned Carol to do this picture because my mother-in-law's maiden name was Cardinal. The other original is a captivating, red-headed girl with a butterfly perched on her fingers. This vivid watercolor dances with life and is displayed in my guest room.

I also have a few well-known prints hung throughout my home that please me. One, entitled *On Dreamland's Border,* is a Bessie Pease Gutman illustration of a baby whose heavy eyes are about to close. It's in a round frame and hangs in my upstairs hall. I was smitten with how much this baby looked like my eldest son, Marty, at the same age. In fact, a number of friends, on seeing the picture, have asked if it were he. Bessie's ability to capture the gentle, innocent side of childhood is endearing.

My guest room proudly houses a Thomas Kinkade English cottage. His gifted touch with light causes the windows to glow on this canvas of *Julianne's Cottage,* which was once the home of Beatrix Potter. I had a light mounted on the frame so that in the evening one could observe from the bed the illumination of the cottage and the sunset.

Down the short hall that leads to the door that goes nowhere, I have hung a series of prints by G. Harvey. My most prized Harvey is entitled *Of One Spirit.* Dr. James Dobson presented this print to me at a Focus on the Family chapel service, which makes the artwork especially meaningful. Each year, Mr. Harvey has created a new picture and donated it to Focus. The prints produced from it are numbered, and the funds raised are used to assist Focus in its many life-changing endeavors.

I also enjoy investing in up-and-coming artists, and it's especially sweet to me when they are local. I purchased an acrylic painting by Jane Donavan of our downtown main street in Brighton, Michigan. Since I love our charming street and have walked it and shopped it now for more than thirty years, this picture delights me.

My bedroom touts a lovely old print that continues to charm my heart. It's of a mother with her two children at a fountain in the park. Les and I purchased it at an antique store in Mackinac City many years ago. The print appears to be from the late 1800s.

Because I am such a picture fanatic, I also do seasonal hangings. I store framed prints under the beds, and every once in awhile do a big switcheroo. It gives the rooms a fresh look and allows me to enjoy a greater variety of prints. Winter scenes are a real temptation for me, but once I'm into spring, I enjoy storing the snow prints.

Some pictures I never take down. For instance, a meadow scene of cows by the water's edge that once hung over my grandmother's fireplace now hangs by mine. It's not valuable to anyone but my family; however, for us it's a prized possession. My mom displayed a large, antique Dutch picture in her home, and about fifteen years ago she presented it to me. I was tickled. I have since obtained at an auction another antique Dutch picture that I really enjoy … and we're not even Dutch. All three prints hang in our living room. From time to time I may move them into other rooms, but they are always displayed somewhere in our house.

I have a floral watercolor I painted. Yep, that's right, me. It's a true original. I keep it under my bed … all the time. It's really not bad, but I haven't had the courage to hang it. Once in awhile I pull it out, dust it off, and then put it away again. Maybe one day …

The point to the description of my home's hangings is that you don't have to own a Rembrandt to make your home more picturesque. Wonderful pieces of art, including posters, when framed, enhance a room and can bring you years of viewing pleasure. Art is very personal. Buy what pleases your eye, but don't limit yourself to one type of art. Expand your art savvy. Take a class, peruse the library, interview an area artist, and meander through a museum. Oh, yes, saunter through the woods, survey a sunrise, count falling stars, polish a  shell, sketch a bluebird, and dust off a daffodil. I promise you will be inspired, for these are often the things of which great art is made.

If you're a nonartist like me, venture out of your comfort zone and paint your own Monet, Rockwell, or Engelbreit. If nothing else, you could hang your finished work, say, under your bed. I have a pen and ink drawing by my Aunt Ada. It's small and not especially skillfully done, yet, because I know she did it, I prize it. My aunt died before I was born, and her little art piece helps me to know her a bit better. I also have a napkin on which my dad sketched a cartoon figure years ago. Dad was a doodler. And this doodler's daughter is delighted to have that tiny treasure. So, see? You don't have to be a Kinkade, a Gutman, or a Harvey to leave behind art for someone who loves you. Hmm, perhaps one day a relative will check out my small offering, and maybe, just maybe, she will even hang it on her wall, or under…

Another way I include pictures in my home is through photographs. I've framed family and friends and placed them in mini groupings scattered about our rooms. Upstairs I have a cluster of friends displayed—old friends, new friends, young friends, and ministry friends, who smile at me daily. The pictures remind me of the rich blessings of friendship and promote my prayers and praise on their behalf and mine.

Our stairwell is developing into a family gallery. I have gradually been framing old prints from Les' family and mine. It has taken years to obtain pictures (finagling family members can take a long time), and the cost of matting and framing adds up quickly. We borrowed a few of the photographs and had prints made from them. Others were dug out of storage sheds, basements, and attics. Some relatives' photos are sort of scary. (I wonder if future generations will say the same of us? I know

I've already guffawed over a few of my own pics.) But, I must say, our relatives' visual presence has added to the interest factor as you climb our stairs. I like to show off our historical and hysterical crew while helping to give my children and their children a sense of family connectedness.

But regardless how stunning the artwork we hang in our homes, the Master Artist won't be outdone. Last night I was taken by surprise when I looked into the skies. One of the most beautiful sunsets I have seen transformed the firmament into a breathtaking canvas. Pinks and peaches turned to vivid oranges and mauves and then turned back again. Tufts of cotton clouds absorbed the peach colors while drifting across the periwinkle skies. Then suddenly rays of light from the setting sun exploded the colors into an electrifying spectacle. I became very still as I watched these heavenly dynamics lest I miss some of it, and I tried to record the experience in my soul. I decided, even as I watched, that words could never capture what my eyes had seen. It was one of those "you'd have to be there" moments. Neighbors were pouring out of their homes to take it in while some ran for cameras and video cams. The changing displays lasted about twenty minutes, but the impact on those of us who attended this unexpected performance will stay with us for a very long time.

That work of art, my friends, was commissioned by our Designer. The One who created each of us as a one-of-a-kind masterpiece. The Lord views us through a lens of mercy and frames us in his generous love that we might be connected to him and his other children forever. Now, that's family, and, yes, that's art in its finest form.

$\mathcal{P}$oints of View

$\mathcal{I}$ was, for the umpteenth time, rearranging my living room when a thought struck me. I always stand to make decorating decisions, but during 90 percent of the time I'm in those rooms I actually will be seated. This prompted me to arrange some things in ways and positions I hadn't tried previously. I moved from chair to couch to table to bed throughout my home, asking myself, "What do you see?" Then I decided if it pleased me from different positions—sitting and standing. Adjustments in heights and angles cast new light on each room. It's a new point of view.

Sometimes it's easier to shed new decorating light on a friend's abode that we occasionally visit than on our own homes. I've even noticed, when I've been on the road for awhile, that the away time has given me a visual break from my environment, allowing me to see my surroundings from a different perspective. But sometimes I run out of new angles and need someone to help me "see." Like me, you may have discovered, after you've changed things around time after time, you begin to think you've used up all your options. That's when another's point of view can be your best choice.

Awhile back I asked two friends, Ann and Linda, to decorate a shelf in my dining

room. The end result was lovely. I had to purchase only a holder for a cup and saucer and two small doilies. Everything else I already owned and had tucked away in cupboards.

Initially, I found it difficult to ask for help because I enjoy doing my own decorating as well as receiving any accolades. But my schedule was demanding, my energy was dwindling, and my unfinished room was a constant drain on my brain. So I pressed past my pride and asked others for help. What I ended up with was a visual delight. Ann and Linda's points of view enhanced my dining room and relieved me of the pressure to complete the project.

Along with friends, home or interior designers can be valuable resources. An expert can size up a situation and list or create for you innovative additions or necessary subtractions.

I had an interior designer come into my home to measure some windows for shades. When she walked into my long and narrow kitchen, she eyed my table at the end of the room and casually mentioned I should try turning it at an angle. We made the adjustment, and I could hardly believe my eyes. That five-inch change made the table look more inviting, made it easier to walk past, and caused the room to appear better balanced. I also loved that I didn't have to purchase six hundred items (and my husband says I exaggerate!) to achieve the desired result.

We have an affordable service in our town run by a couple of gifted gals. They will come into your home (they send you away for a few hours), take what you already own, and create a whole new look for you. What a great pick-me-up during a season in which you just don't have the time or inclination to make much-needed changes. Or perhaps decorating isn't your forte, and you don't want to be bothered with details. I've always thought the service would make a wonderful gift for someone who could use an encouraging lift or who was ill and needed a fresh atmosphere to recuperate in.

If you're like me, you're deeply affected by your surroundings. When my home is in order, I seem better able to sort out the rest of my life. When it's attractive, I'm more motivated, encouraged, and even relaxed. But when my home is suffering from the doldrums, I tend to trudge about in melancholy response. Keeping my environment snapping, crackling, and popping with interest is for me an emotional investment.

Let's say the budget doesn't allow for a professional's point of view, you've just moved to a new community, you don't have family or friends to make suggestions, and you don't have an eye for decorating. Go to the market (or library) and breeze through a few home-oriented magazines until you find a couple of appealing rooms. Then ask yourself what it is about the rooms that you like best: placement of furnishings, color of walls, style of furniture, or types of accessories? Make notes of what pleases you. Use those pictures and notes as your decorating guide.

Paint is one of the most inexpensive yet transforming changes, if you do it yourself. Stenciling is still a popular option and is a creative choice for some areas of your home. I've seen some delightful stenciling done above sinks, in utility rooms, and on porches. I think for longevity the key is a free-flowing stencil that appears more like a freehand work of art. Although the ordered, straight-across stencils have a real appeal to people who appreciate all their i's dotted and their t's crossed, I tend to be a little more relaxed and artsy in my approach.

Today's walls are often treated like a canvas for all types of creative expressions: wallpapering, ragging, splattering, newspapering, sponging, fauxing … and the list continues to grow. We can get an expert's point of view and step-by-step painting directions via the television home-and-garden programs. Also check out resources such as the library, home extension classes, community education, park district courses, and paint craft stores. Most of these resources will only cost you some time and a few supplies.

I confess that on several occasions others' viewpoints have saved me from some decorating disasters. To my great relief, I'm told even professionals sometimes misjudge a project and have to backtrack from their original ideas.

Recently, I hung some window scarves in a little retreat condo we were staying in out West. Friends who dropped by were speechless when they saw the window coverings. These people were usually expressive so I wondered if perhaps they disliked my choice. Well, it turned out they despised it. They suggested the gauzy, swirled material might have worked better in King Solomon's concubine quarters. We all ended up laughing long and hard over my "camel curtains."

I guess I knew even before I purchased the scarves that they might not be right because I asked the clerk several times if she was certain I could return them. And after they were hung, I felt uneasy each time I entered the room, but I thought I just needed to live with them for awhile. My friends assured me no one needed to live with them … ever.

To tell you the truth, I was so stretched by my schedule that I just wanted the windows covered so I could get on with other pressing demands. After I swagged the scarves across my windows, I kept asking folks for their evaluation, which was a sure indication of my insecurity. So, decorating rule number one is: Don't make selections when you are feeling ragtag and just want the job over with. Listen to your uneasiness; trust your gut instinct. Rule number two: Have in your circle of friends those whose opinion you regard and who will be honest. Rule number three: Don't give up something you really like because others don't care for it, and don't hang onto a decorating mistake to protect your pride. (Yes, I returned the curtains.)

Just as I have benefited from others' decorating insights, I have also learned to lean in to hear the Lord's counsel. Talk about a different perspective! He states in Scripture that "my thoughts are not your thoughts, neither are your ways my ways" (Isaiah 55:8). Which means to me that if I don't hear from him, I could miss the whole point of my successes, my failures, my losses, and my gains. We are challenged with the truth, "What good will it be for a man if he gains the whole world, yet forfeits his soul?" (Matthew 16:26). Meanwhile, 1 Corinthians provides me with invaluable decorating directions. It tells me that love makes the most lasting impact. And that faith and hope are invaluable in this life. Therefore, while we are adorning our environments, let's remember to wear our faith with flair, hold onto hope, and lavish love … especially at home.

Heritage

My mom is a bridge builder. Her bridges have been somewhat like the Golden Gate in that they span great distances—but over generations instead of water. She has helped her family to hang on to its heritage via pictures, stories, and furnishings.

Mom taught me to appreciate antiques and family history by her demonstrated passion for both. As far back as I can remember, she carefully cared for family memorabilia. Perhaps one reason she has valued it is that so little of it is available. In fact, one of the ways she has made up for the deficit is to purchase lovely old pieces to pass down from generation to generation. Many of those investments now add richness to my surroundings.

Most of my grandmotherly treasures are from my dad's mom, whom we called Mamaw. Mamaw and Papaw had very little, but what I have of theirs is precious to me. Throughout my home you'll find her treadle sewing machine, wooden icebox, trunk, doll, hand-tied quilt, box of pictures, school slate, ring for a bull's nose, a wall hanging, some small items that belonged to my Aunt Ada (Mamaw's only daughter, who died before I knew her), and a Bible we believe Mamaw had since her childhood. What an eclectic collection!

My interest in family "old stuff" gradually grew within me as I tired of newfangled gizmos and began to appreciate the quality of yesterday. Besides, mementos are chock-full of memories. Now, the older I get, the more old appears gold to me.

Today I become downright slushy when it comes to family keepsakes. Somehow I feel more connected to my relatives as I integrate their history into the making of our own.

More often than I can count people tell me about discarded family items they now long to have, not for the monetary gain but for a tangible way to hold on to their history and for the memories stirred. I don't think a price tag can be placed on personal history.

My dad was a Sealtest milkman who worked out of the Detroit Creamery delivering to stores and later house to house in the suburbs until the creamery closed in the early 1970s. Our home was always loaded with dairy products: sour cream, cottage cheese, half-and-half, ice cream, buttermilk, and, of course, endless bottles of whole milk.

Several years ago I began to collect Sealtest milk bottles marked with the Detroit Creamery insignia. The hunt for the bottles was fun for Les and me. Over the years we had both helped my dad deliver milk; Les even more than I had. With each find came a fresh flood of fond memories. Along the way I also picked up some Sealtest extras including a large tin spoon, a light-up sign, recipe booklets, calendars, and rulers.

I now have quite an accumulation of milk bottles. In fact, my husband said we would either have to find something else to collect or open a creamery ourselves. Initially, when I started to collect the bottles, they could be purchased for 25 to 50 cents each. Now they sell for $2 to $15 each.

I have discovered different ways to productively incorporate the glass bottles into our home. Some are simply clustered in baskets sitting hither and yon as though the milkman has dropped them off, while others work as flower vases, candleholders, creamers, or syrup pitchers. They also work nicely for rooting plants, quenching the thirst of potted plants, and mixing plant potions.

I own half-gallon, quart, pint, and half-pint bottles. The half-pints are my favorites because they are so versatile and because Half-Pint was the nickname my dad and brother gave me when I was growing up. What sweet remembrances.

One of my earliest memories is of the ice man delivering a grand chunk of ice—sparkling in the sun like the Hope Diamond and held securely with his giant ice tongs—to Mamaw's back porch. There he would deposit it in her icebox. Mamaw was the only person I knew who owned such a fascinating contraption.

After the ice was placed into the top of the four-foot wooden box, you could retrieve your milk, eggs, and other perishables through a lower door. When my parents finally were able to convince Mamaw to move on up to a real refrigerator, she kept her icebox. I'm grateful that she did because today the icebox charms my entry, providing me with extra storage and tender recollections of my grandmother, my childhood, and a seemingly simpler lifestyle.

Here are a few other ways I have incorporated family treasures: I have an old fountain pen of my Aunt Ada's displayed in an inkwell on my desk. Every Christmas we

dig out my grandmother's emerald-green tumblers to enhance our holiday mealtime. I have a childhood doll, Dydee, sitting in my office; she is dressed in handmade clothes my mom stitched and crocheted for me at my birth. My brother's bronzed baby shoes serve as bookends for old schoolbooks, some that belonged to my dad.

Not all of our old stuff, though, is from our families. When we enjoy the quality and workmanship of an old piece, we are willing to build some of our own history with our purchases. Just after Les and I moved into my dream-come-true home, we decided to give ourselves a housewarming gift. Wasn't that thoughtful? We had spotted an antique oak buffet with beveled oval mirror and were certain it needed to live in our dining room. We saw this buffet not only as a lovely addition for us, but also as a piece that would increase in value, to be passed along to future generations.

Now, a word about my dream-come-true home, which we chose partly because of its sense of history. I have always longed for a snug home in a cozy community. A place where children still decorate their bicycle spokes with playing cards secured with clothespins. Where they decorate their dogs with top hats and huge bow ties and then parade down Main Street. And where you know the store owners by name and they know you. I wanted our storybook home to be infused with surprises, both old and new. I desired at least one curved archway, cove ceilings, a porch or two, and a generous yard. We feel so blessed to have found this darling home in a community we love. The ambiance pleases our hearts, nurtures our souls, and provides a sense of belonging.

Those are the same benefits that accrue to those who find ways to incorporate their family's heritage into everyday life. I've had the delight of helping others dig out family treasures and discover ways to make them more visible. One friend had a wonderful collection of pocket watches we displayed on the wall among pictures. Another friend used her mother's brooches to hold back the lace curtains in her bedroom. In another home an old smoking stand now serves as a handy bedside stand for book, glasses, and water decanter.

My friend Ginny had her grandmother's sterling baby spoon made into a ring for her daughter, Erin. One day Erin will pass it down to her daughter, Rachel. That will make four generations of sterling ties—I like that. Ginny also has incorporated an old cream separator in her side garden.

What family goodies are in your cupboards? Perhaps it's time to discover ways to infuse your home with your family's history.

The reminders of those who have gone before us can hearten our steps and promote a sense of family solidity, needed not only in our physical families but also in a spiritual sense. One of my favorite stability verses is from the psalmist David when he proclaims, "He set my feet upon a rock making my footsteps firm" (Psalm 40:2b, NASB).

We are offered a firm foundation in Christ. He becomes our bridge to God, and we become a part of his family. We are then encouraged to familiarize ourselves with those who have gone before us in the Lord through studying Scripture. In Hebrews 11, we glimpse some of our spiritual family's history, beginning with Abel, Enoch, Abraham, and Sarah.

How does it assist us to bridge the centuries with our Bible family? For me, when I read of Abel's demise, I'm jolted into the reality that injustice will always be with us. That helps me with the onslaught of the evening news that reeks of humankind's cruelty.

As I study Sarah's life, I see her triumphant faith and her dismal failures, which help me accept my own inconsistencies. I take heart at her courage, her charity, and her long-awaited answered prayers. I identify with her doubts, and I am convicted by her harsh treatment of Hagar. I am reminded that jealousy creates strife.

Knowing my spiritual family helps me treasure their lessons and learn from their lives. How wonderful to gain from the rich resources of yesterday as we live out the grand adventure of today. So decorate your home with history and your heart with charity that you might become a bridge builder for future generations. "The Lord is the portion of my inheritance and my cup; thou dost support my lot. The lines have fallen to me in pleasant places; indeed my heritage is beautiful to me" (Psalm 16:5-6, NASB).

Reading Corners

I didn't become an avid reader until I was a young adult. Then, out of desperation for answers in my life, I developed an insatiable appetite for books. Books became the rope of hope that helped pull me through emotionally troubled years. They offered me supportive companionship, nonthreatening advice, much-needed humor, and life-changing principles. I became such a book fanatic that eventually I opened a small bookstore in my home to feed my voracious habit and to encourage others to read.

Most of my early book reading was how-to books because I needed to know how to in most areas of my life. Today, I still love an insightful, directive book, but my reading circle is much broader. I have a passion for children's books, novels, art, cookbooks, poetry, and beautifully presented gift books on homes and gardens. My family has learned that, to delight me at holiday time, just give me a book. Or present me with a gift coupon that allows me to spend part of a day selecting just the right volume. This doubles my pleasure, as the time in a good bookstore is a gift in and of itself. Besides, I relish the hunt.

In my home, book corners developed quite naturally as I sought out quiet places to peruse mounting stacks of books. To prepare a reading corner takes very little

My friend Ruthann and I often book browse.

effort and yet brings long-term benefits and pleasure. Locate a corner and then cozy it up. See? That's simple. You'll need a comfy chair (or a lot of accommodating pillows), a three-way reading lamp (I prefer adjustable floor lamps), a small table (to hold tea and scones, of course), a soft throw (to, uh, throw), and a basket of delicious reading material (to ingest).

I have several favorite reading spots scattered throughout my home that beckon me. Of course, it doesn't take much to convince me to sit a spell and leaf through some captivating books. The blue and white loveseat in my office sports a half-dozen paunchy pillows and often whispers my name. Or so it would seem as I leave my office chair and tiptoe across the room to sink down into the couch's friendly surroundings. A myriad of books awaits me, stacked on the floor close by. A person can get too comfortable, though, and the next thing you know you're in siesta land.

Our sunny guest room offers a wonderful corner to curl up in with, say, a copy of L.M. Montgomery's *Anne of Green Gables*, C.S. Lewis' *The Screwtape Letters*, or Philip Yancey's *What's So Amazing About Grace?*

The chair in this room is one of my favorites. Actually, I decorated the guest room around it to give the chair a fitting space of its own. Built close to the floor (as is its owner), the chair offers corpulent cushions covered in heart-cheering fabric. The arms are chubby and add to the comfort. The room is a profusion of blues, yellows, and whites, which pleases my eyes. I have a three-way floor lamp, purchased at a barn sale, behind my chair and, next to it, a small antique table acquired at an auction. A basketful of reading selections sits nearby, and a footstool provides hours of propped reading comfort.

My dining room has a high-backed chair that I will nestle into from time to time. The lamp on the buffet isn't the best for long-term viewing so I just do little snippets of reading there. My desk and my kitchen table make great spots for serious study while my front porch is the ideal place to peruse my magazines.

Where do you do your reading? What about your family? Do you have offerings readily available to change your life and your loved ones' outlook?

Even if you can't afford major book investments, you can still read plenty. In the early years, when I had no book budget, I borrowed books. I remain grateful to those who had extensive libraries and shared them with me.

Not everyone is willing to loan books, and, may I say, with good reason. Often a borrowed book becomes so absorbed into our homes that we forget it was borrowed or that it now shores up the broken leg on our bedroom dresser. Also, some relaxed readers may absentmindedly dog-ear pages, causing the book's meticulous owner to growl in dismay. Some borrowers may take the liberty of writing their insights in the margins, or even worse, feel led to loan the borrowed book to yet someone else. Can you tell this bothers me?

If you feel sharing your books is a ministry, which it certainly can be, you may want to set up a loaning system. To be a good book lender, take five minutes next time you are at an office supply store to purchase index cards and a card holder. Keep this mini-file on your library shelf. Then, when you loan a book, ask the borrowee to write

down the title, date, and her signature. Filling out the card reminds the person you really do want that book back. Then, every three months or so, check your file to see if loaned selections have made it home. It's not wrong to protect your investment and extend your future outreach; besides, people respect people who respect themselves.

To be a good book borrower, treat the books in your care as though they are gifts for someone else. Also write down on your daily calendar a note to return the book by a certain date and the name of the person you borrowed it from. I have more than once forgotten who loaned me a certain book and have had to poll all my friends.

If a book is damaged while in your possession (recently a leaky bottle of water saturated the corner pages of a paperback book I had borrowed), replace it with a new copy. Then return both to the owner in case the original held some nostalgic place in her heart or contained some important notations.

Slipping a pretty bookmark in a borrowed book before returning it is a thoughtful way to say you appreciate the lender's generosity. Also, a short note listing the book's highlights for you would be a thoughtful addition, if you feel so led.

Books should never take the place of relationships, but I confess more than one book has become my lifetime friend. Books that were placed in my hands during crucial times in my life prompted me to take the next step in my personal journey. Come along and allow me to introduce you to some of my favorites…

One of the first books to make an impact on my life was *The Christian's Secret of a Happy Life* by Hannah Whithall Smith. Her chapter, "Is God in Everything?" was invaluable for me. I remember tape-recording that chapter and then replaying it until I took the stabilizing truth into the marrow of my bones, including this thought:

> God does not order the wrong thing, but he uses it for our blessing; just as he used the cruelty of Joseph's wicked brethren, and the false accusations of Pharaoh's wife. In short, this way of seeing our Father in everything makes life one long thanksgiving, and gives a rest of heart, and more than that, a gaiety of spirit, that is unspeakable.

Another classic that has continued to influence my life is Oswald Chambers' *My Utmost for His Highest*. How such a young man could have been so wise is beyond me (he died at the age of forty-two). His stenographer wife took copious notes of her husband's sermons, which today, in the form of devotionals, bless millions. Year after year I read his writings and have yet to exhaust his deeply layered insights.

In fact, many years ago I presented a copy of *My Utmost* to my treasured friend Florence Littauer. Each year, using a different color, she has highlighted fresh revelations, giving her copy a rainbow appearance. It has been a pot-of-gold experience as she, like me, continues to be enriched by Oswald Chambers.

Morning and Evening by Charles Spurgeon is another unforgettable devotional. It begins with his challenge: "Let January open with joy in the Lord and December close with gladness in Jesus." *Morning and Evening* feeds my artistic soul as well as my spirit. Spurgeon's masterful verbiage is thrilling to read as he leads one from tears of conviction to peals of praise. For example:

No joy can excel that of the soldier of Christ: Jesus reveals Himself so graciously, and gives such sweet refreshment, that the warrior feels more calm and peace in his daily strife than others in their hours of rest.

Also, I appreciate the devotional's design that offers a reading for morning and evening. What a pleasing way to enter into and close each day.

One of my all-time favorite books is by Calvin Miller, entitled *The Table of Inwardness*. A thin book, it has had a voluminous impact on me. Mr. Miller explores the barrenness of busyness with understanding and conviction.

Once we become masters of our own schedule, we will be able to approach God in peace.

Those who have not learned this come to God as they do everything else … late. They rush into the great white throne, a tornado of hurriedness. They blurt out their confessions and whisk on to the next appointment, glad that they have managed to work God into their blustery schedules.

In contrast, Miller invites us to experience the satisfaction that is ours when we make time to dine with our Savior.

Spiritual inwardness is a longing after Christ. It is a table set for us with food not prepared by human hands. The Host is there. He is ready. There are only two chairs at the table, and there we may delight to sit and sup with the Son of God.

My tendency is to flit away hours and then grieve my loss of time and opportunities. *The Table of Inwardness* has been a kind yet strong reminder of what matters and what lasts.

Another current author who thrills me with his grace-filled pen is Ken Gire. Mr. Gire's tender writings (*Intimate Moments with the Savior, Intense Moments, Instructional Moments, Incredible Moments*) never fail to deeply move me. When read aloud, they are even more elegant. His sensitive nature, combined with his wise musings, is woven throughout, causing his writings to resound like a sweet aria of faith.

And *sweet* is the word I would use to describe *Toot and Puddle,* a children's book written by artist Holly Hobbie. Actually, add to *sweet* the words *darling, adorable,* and *endearing.* This story about two pigs from Woodcock Pocket demonstrates how to stay friends even when you're very different. The book charmed my socks off and won the hearts of all my friends as well.

Ken Gire has also written a children's book I am wild about, *The Adventures of Big Thicket.* Unfortunately, it has gone out of print, so you may have to root around to unearth this treasure via used book stores, church libraries, and collectors. The joy-producing adventure with exceptional art makes the book a must for kids of all ages. I giggled my way through this one, all the time wishing I had written it.

Speaking of wishing I had written it, have you experienced *Redeeming Love,* a novel by Francine Rivers? It's a breathtaking portrayal of God's pursuing love of a prostitute. I was held spellbound as Angel repeatedly ran from the only One who could redeem her shame-filled life and awaken her deadened heart.

I gave my friend Ginny a copy of *Redeeming Love* and her husband, Alan, absconded with it and read it straight through. He said reading the story of Mr. Hosea's unconditional love for Angel stirred Alan to love his wife more fervently. He now heartily recommends the novel to all his guy friends.

I have to admit there is no end to my book list because I have benefited from so many. And I am a firm believer that if you gain one new insight from a book, respond to conviction, experience emotional relief, deepen your faith, or have your outlook buoyed, your investment of time and money was an overwhelming success.

Of course, heading my book list is the masterpiece that provides the most benefits. The Author wrote this magnificent manifesto of faith so we might be changed internally and eternally. His theme is love, and his desire is for our best interest.

"'For I know the plans that I have for you,' declares the Lord, 'plans for welfare and not for calamity to give you a future and a hope'" (Jeremiah 29:11, NASB).

I place Bibles throughout my home so one is always at my fingertips. I enjoy different translations as well as different sizes. If you haven't tried *The Message* by Eugene Peterson, it will be to your soul like a fresh breeze on a stifling day. I appreciate the teaching benefits in *The Living Insights Study Bible* and *The International Inductive Study Bible*. I enjoy the *New American Standard* version for study but also check out the *New International*. And for me there is nothing like a meditative read from the King James version, which is what I cut my spiritual teeth on. The *thees* and *thous* might slow down a reader's progress, but they sure add a poetic sense that I appreciate.

I love that the Word of God is full of intrigue, love, mystery, family, prophecy, heresy, royalty, destiny, and much more. My favorite books are Genesis, Exodus, Isaiah, John, James, and oh, yes, Psalms and Proverbs. Certainly Ruth and Jonah are important to me. And of course Philippians … hmm, I guess I love them all.

What are your favorites? Betcha can't pick just one. Come join me in a reading corner with the Scriptures for the adventure of our lives as we read words that will reverberate throughout eternity.

"Heaven and earth will pass away, but my words will never pass away" (Mark 13:31).

Reading corners with books tucked in baskets or displayed on bookshelves are valuable additions to any home. Books can strengthen our minds, enhance our characters, improve our vocabularies, keep us informed, and make us more versatile conversationalists. In *Shadowlands*, a movie about C.S. Lewis, there is a line that I can say "amen" to: "We read to know that we are not alone." Books should never be our only friends, but keeping company with books is a friendly thing to do.

Wayside Room

As a youngster, I was ecstatic when Mom announced we were going to have houseguests. I thrived on the influx of added personalities and the flurry of activity that occurred because of their presence. Besides, company meant Mom would roll out the feather bed and tuck it and me in some cozy nook. She would fluff the feathers to create the perfect rise by heartily shaking the pinstriped pillow bed until it was pregnant with softness. Then I would sink into it, and the downy sides would engulf me with tenderness, like a mama hen encircling her chick. Oh, yes, I loved having company.

Guests also caused our dinner table to overflow with Mom's best offerings. She would slather her roasts in their natural juices and then transform the juices into luscious gravies. We would liberally ladle the gravy onto her homemade baking powder biscuits and mounds of fluffy mashed potatoes. Yum … and that was just the beginning. The end, dessert, was the absolute best. Alternating layers of cooked vanilla pudding, sliced bananas, and vanilla wafers were peaked with mile-high meringue that was toasted to perfection. Big-time yum!

When guests were to arrive, our refrigerator teemed with endless possibilities and the cookie bin nearly burst with fresh choices. (Actually, my favorites were store-

bought Pinwheels and devil's food cookies.) But nothing was tastier than company breakfast southern style. I would somersault from my bed on those mornings without being coaxed. I'm not sure if my energy was the result of waking to the aroma of bacon wafting through the house and encircling my bed or anticipating the fresh conversation and laughter that our guests would bring to the table. Dipping Mom's biscuits into pools of thick milk gravy and the yolk from perfectly prepared eggs while visiting around the table remains for me a delicious recollection.

I am not Child-like, as in Julia, so my guests don't enjoy milk gravy or homemade biscuits (although I do cook a lovely waffle), but I try to make up for those losses with a nurturing environment designed especially for my visitors. When possible, I like to place a framed photo of my guest next to her bed or possibly in her washroom. That personalization lets her know I have prepared the room with her in mind.

My guest also will find a note of welcome on her pillow expressing our delight in having her in our home. (It may be a rarity today, in this computer, e-mail, form-letter world, but for me a handwritten note holds great appeal.) I try to select a note card that fits my guest's tastes or that coordinates with the room.

Flowers and chocolates make thoughtful additions … unless your guest has allergies to one or both. (Beware, potpourri can also cause problems for allergic folks.) I try to make simple floral arrangements. In fact, in the wayside room, I keep a cobalt-blue water bottle tied at the neck with a pale yellow grosgrain ribbon. Before a visitor arrives, I slip in a couple of tulips, daisies, or roses for a welcoming touch. If flowers are an aggravant for a guest, I have a lovely faux bouquet of lilies of the valley that appear sweetly authentic.

Speaking of sweet, I enjoy selecting Godiva chocolates to set next to the bed and a small tin of butterscotch or peppermints for the dresser to appease my sweet-toothed friends. A water decanter and a glass sit on the bedstead for those evening pills and midnight sips. When I'm really on my morning toes and hear my guest stirring, I place a stemmed goblet of juice with a good morning note at her door. I tap and dash so as not to be too intrusive in morning rituals. An area newspaper also is nice to offer to acquaint your guest with your community.

I've made sure night-lights dot the landscape (or should I say "footscape"?) from bed to bath in an attempt to take the mystery out of the journey. I also have an over-the-door ironing board on the closet door and an iron at my company's fingertips (on the closet shelf) to assist in tidying up suitcase-crumpled attire. A large basket overflows with towels and washcloths, with an additional supply in the washroom—I like to provide far more than my guest will need.

I try to keep the following items in the guest bathroom: extra tissue products, a plunger, air freshener, hot water bottle, thermometer, toothbrush, toothpaste, and headache tablets. For those unexpected times we lose power (usually during storms) I have learned to keep an oil lamp or a candle (with matches) available for guests.

I display offerings of reading materials throughout the guest room. A few friendly stacks of showy books (art, gardens, etc.) are maintained on the trunk, and a basket of eclectic choices (novels, devotionals, poetry, children's) nestle next to the reading chair. I keep current issues of several magazines (such as *Romantic Homes* and *Home Companion*) on the bed tray and in the vanity area. I may even press a Post-It note on a magazine's cover to alert my guest to a couple of articles I think might be of personal interest to her. A few classics lie about, such as *Hind's Feet on High Places*, poems of Emily Dickinson, and Winnie-the-Pooh books.

The high-backed, spoon-carved oak guest bed is congested with pillows of all sizes. I suggest my company stash them behind the reading chair, if they choose not to fuss with the fluffy array. Another comforting factor I like to offer is a lock on the door, which affords a greater sense of security and privacy. We had a telephone jack added to

the room, and just before guests arrive, I plug in a phone for their convenience.

I warn guests about any noises that might be disconcerting to them, like the not-so-distant trains in the middle of the night. Also, the natural settling sounds of our old house as it moans its way through the night and groans its way into the new day (rather like its owners) could cause some guests discomfort.

I've heard it said that a person should spend the night in her own guest room to understand what to provide for visitors. My friend tried that at her home and immediately purchased a new mattress.

While personally testing your wayside room is a good teacher, my most influential learning experiences have been staying in other people's homes. Because of my speaking ministry, I often reside for short intervals in total strangers' homes. I've been fortunate through the years to stay with people who have the gift of hospitality. Although a few awkward situations have occurred (such as fleas and dirty sheets), the good far outweighs the bad, and some of my hostesses have become cherished friends.

For years, whenever I have traveled to southern California, I have had an ongoing invitation to stay in the Lukei home. Ginny Lukei offered to drive and house me for an event nine years ago, and we have been heart-fast friends ever since. Ginny not only offers me a cheery room, personalized care, and her friendship, but she also lovingly incorporates me into her family. What a gift to be connected to a family and a functioning home while I'm away from my own.

One of the endearing things Ginny does for me while I'm visiting is to bake potato rolls. They are to die for! Well, okay, maybe not die, but you are aware, as you devour them, that you must always have Ginny's potato rolls in your life. Ginny is one awesome cook. She claims her recipes are simple, but I think she has a Galloping Gourmet thumb (similar to a green thumb but doused in olive oil and garlic, with just a pinch of parsley).

Because Ginny and I have spent so much time together over the years in her home, at conferences, and in training seminars, we each have learned what delights the other. We both love a present. I'm not talking about bust-the-budget gifts, but those that have been thought through and fit the person. It might be a new tea, a charming magnet, or a handmade card.

Ginny came into my life and offered me her home when I didn't know her. She served me unselfishly and creatively. She kept her door open so I could return as often as I needed. She expanded my family by offering me hers. And she has been willing to walk through the good and the not-so-good times as a faithful friend. Ginny has been like Jesus. Little did I realize, when she offered me her guest room, how important that would be in my life.

We never know who may pass our way, who might need shelter, whom we will entertain, or who will entertain us. In the book of Hebrews, we are told, "Do not neglect to show hospitality to strangers, for by this some have entertained angels without knowing it" (13:2, NASB). I don't know if I have housed any angels yet (although my guests have been heavenly), but I don't want to miss my chance if one comes my way.

Angel in disguise frocked in friendships coat,
Come and rest awhile, read my welcome note.

For here you are safe to eat, drink, and sleep,
Sheltered in our home, promises to keep.

The promise is His spoken from above,
"Take care of strangers, abide in My love."

Angel wings rustle, my heart skips a beat.
At our open door stands someone to greet.

$\mathcal{P}$layful Reminders

$\mathcal{I}$n our home, we strongly believe that if you don't laugh you won't live … at least not joyfully. Life can be difficult enough without adding intensity by our uptight reactions. I'm chuckling as I write this for I am often the one who is intense, especially when an approaching deadline is bearing down on my last nerve. But I have found laughter and fun to be just the implements to untie my taut emotions, clear my stuffy brain, and improve my stifled relationships.

When the Lord designed us with the capacity to laugh aloud, I don't think it was a last-minute thought or a divine oops. For we know he makes no mistakes. I believe the Lord gave us laughter as a physical and emotional way to get out from under life's drudgery.

Recently, I visited an art gallery with my laugh-filled friends Luci Swindoll and Mary Graham. As we ambled through the gallery, we stifled our laughter so as not to disrupt the other gallerygoers. We passed one stoic guard after another who observed our behavior. Heavy black lines marked off foot boundaries and woe to the one who stepped over them. Once Luci merely leaned forward to make an observation and was immediately scolded. We had a great time, but it was a relief

after a few hours to leave and have an uproarious giggle-fest.

I'm grateful our homes are not meant to be museums. At my house, no guards make sure you don't touch my property, nor do heavy lines suggest you mustn't step over. There are no uplifted brows if you laugh heartily and frequently—especially if I'm in on it.

I'm not suggesting a home have no guidelines. I'm against polo, jousting, archery, and sumo wrestling in my living room. As in all things, moderation is wisdom.

For instance, bed jumping is not wise but, if I recall correctly, a lot of fun. I'm not recommending it, just recollecting it. In fact, the safest way to deal with this childhood need is to put an old mattress on a carpeted surface and let the kids jump till the cows come home or the kids wear out. Easier on you, easier on the kids. And you'll love the sounds that emanate through your home. (May your home always resound with laughter.) Your greatest challenge will be to refrain from joining them. Then again, maybe you should. Who knows, a little sky diving might lift your spirits as well.

I love playful reminders in and around homes to keep us on a cheerful course. My friend Marilyn Meberg told me about her neighbor, who put a large plastic frog next to their shared sidewalk. Every time you walk by, the amphibian replica lets out a "ribbit." Marilyn came home late the day the frog had been "installed" and almost leaped through the side of her house when it greeted her. (She's not fond of amphibians … or the dark.) When she realized what it was, she laughed long and hard, probably as much from relief as from being charmed by its aggravating cuteness.

The Lukeis' home is heavily trafficked because of their gregarious ways. Often they have guests in by the droves for food and fun. So outside their front door they posted a whimsical sign for a company giggle: "Do Duck Inn—Rest and Feast—Man and Beast—Limit 6 to a Bed."

My Aunt Pearl, whose fascination with gizmos kept us tittering, ordered a barking dog recording that was activated when you knocked on her door. Designed to scare off intruders, it served more as a moment of hilarity for those of us who knew her. We understood the only dogs that barked in her life were her aching feet from endless hours of work with convalescents.

My humorous pal Lee has a personable parrot who keeps folks mesmerized. The parrot does (are you ready?) card tricks, plays dead, and sings opera. Of course, the parrot's owner has taken great delight in teaching this mischievous bird how to entertain the troops. And we, the troops, are grateful … and still giggling.

In our home we have fun stuff hither and yon. Why, even our family gallery has a giggle or two. We are delighted to come from a long line of characters. One of my favorite pictures is of my adult mom riding a tricycle. Another is my adult dad getting a playful spanking over his father's knee next to the woodshed. Those photos make me smile and cheer my heart.

In our kitchen you will find a six-inch yellow chalk cat with a chipped ear. I wasn't certain how the injury was incurred until I spotted the three-inch molded (not moldy) mice across the room with nips out of their ears. Here's what I think. One night while we were sleeping Ms. Cat and the twin squeakers had at it! The end result of their scrape was that everybody paid a price. That's all I could figure out since no one, absolutely no one, had any idea how the damage occurred.

Other items in my kitchen make the sides of my mouth turn skyward, including the array of newspaper cartoons regularly arranged on the refrigerator door. Right now I'm featuring Dennis the Menace. Dennis and his buddy are watching his dad bend down to touch his toes. Dennis leans toward his friend and whispers, "I love to hear all those cracklin' sounds." Boy, that one hit close to home (actually my bones do a Rice Krispies concerto).

Along with the cartoons I have magnets on the fridge. My all-time favorite reads, "Mom, I'll always love you, but I'll never forgive you for washing my face with spit on your hanky." We also have a hot plate that says the obvious, "Martha Stewart doesn't live here." (If she did, her cat would have both of its ears.) And thanks to our friend Lisa Harper we have a pig ice cream scoop that oinks as you dollop butter pecan into your bowl (trough).

We also have an assortment of animal antics happening at our house during the Christmas holidays: from a plastic, hula-shaking frog, to a fifteen-inch, stuffed teddy bear who roller-skates to "Edelweiss," to a tin, tricycle-riding duck touting a beanie hat that twirls as he pedals. This comical circus belongs to my husband, who never fails to promote laughter when folks, regardless of their age, see his menagerie.

Life can feel like a three-ringed circus—more going on than we know how to deal with. If we are swept into the tension and get our beanies in a twirling uproar, we will lose perspective and miss out on some good guffaws, which, my friend, never hurt anyone.

Remember, even if only for a moment, that laughter can brighten a cloudy day, lighten a heavy load, and release the tension in a tight moment. Besides, laughter is attractive. Try it and see how much prettier you look. Laughter is appealing. Aren't you drawn to those who laugh easily and well? I am. And laughter is healthy. It infuses our bodies with fresh shipments of life-giving oxygen and pain-relieving endorphins. Besides, shared laughter causes an emotional connectedness that ties us and our memories together in a heartfelt way. So take the time to lighten up your surroundings with a few playful touches and find how pleasing and satisfying it can be as you purpose to live life cheerfully.

P.S. About Ms. Cat and company: I decided not to replace or even repair my feline and her furry fighting friends. Most of life is imperfect, and our attempts to make it flawless are futile and frustrating. So now when I see them in their disrepair it makes me grin with relief and gratitude because, in this earthly existence, stuff will get broken but life will go on. The faulty trio remind me, too, that we are all fractured. And while we may not know who dropped us (or maybe we do), we know the One who accepts us as we are. And that brings me deep-down, knee-slappin', bubbling-over joy.

Serenade

*S*ome of the most soothing sounds during our family's Kentucky vacations were created by the serenade of my grandmother's home. Summer mornings in the South often turned into sultry afternoons, causing the pace of our days to slow dramatically. Family members would sit on Mamaw's shaded porch with tall drafts of iced tea, while others of us would doze lightly inside.

I loved to nap on Mamaw's generous feather bed spread across her aging mattress. There I would dreamily listen in on summer as ice rattled against frosty tumblers, rocking chairs moaned from the strain of guests, and buzzing bees tended to the clover outside the open windows. A small table fan whirred sweet relief while stirring the lace curtains in swishing patterns against the peeling wallpaper. Interspersed in this summer symphony was the melody of the creaking screen door as folks would amble in and out for additional refreshments.

Lulled by the safe sounds of family I would dangle in that delicate space between awake and asleep, every cell of my being at ease. Then ever so gently I would drift off, cradled in a languid lullaby.

All sounds in our spheres, however, are not soothing lullabies. In fact, some can be quite jarring, such as shattering glass or screeching tires. Others are bothersome: the incessant dripping of a faucet, the shrill whistle in the pipes each time the water is turned on, or the neighborhood dog that won't quit howling. I've noticed all homes seem to have varied noises that range from delightful to discordant. And sometimes what is music for one is disruptive to another.

Trains rumble frequently through our little town. For my husband and me the late-night train whistles are like tranquilizers that deepen and sweeten our sleep. But that is not so with guests for whom train clamor has not been a part of their sound repertoire. Perhaps having once lived three houses from the tracks conditioned us for the distant railroad clatter and lonesome whistles that are part of our lives today.

Discordant sounds remind me of a hospital my sister, who was three years old at the time, stayed in undergoing some tests. The medical facility was located on a heavily trafficked road next door to a fire station. The station sirens screamed day and night, putting the patients in a constant emotional state of emergency. Whoever planned that community hadn't listened before they leaped. Between the possibility of living next to clanging trains and screeching sirens, when you consider a house purchase, listen to the sounds surrounding the home as well as in it to make sure you can live with them.

Recently a guest stopped by for a first-time visit. As she walked through my dining room the hardwood floor creaked under her feet. She stopped and applauded the noise. Then she leaned forward and back, replaying the golden oldie that flooded her with thoughts of yesterday. "Oh," she exclaimed, "what a wondrous sound. It brings back a thousand childhood memories."

I wish I could have captured her face on film as it lit up when that noise touched her ears and then her heart. I personally love the lively floor sounds that serve as people-tracking devices, helping me to hone in on everyone's whereabouts. Besides, short of turning on the radio, floor squeaking was one of the only ways I personally had to add music to my home until…

Being musically deficient I can't tell you what a thrill it was for me when friends gave me a Music Maker as a gift. This simple stringed instrument permits one to slide music patterns under the strings, allowing the musically hopeless to pluck out a joyful noise. It has become a tradition during the holidays to leave my Music Maker on the coffee table for guests to tinker with. It has pleased me to see how irresistible that instrument is to passersby. How much satisfaction the instantly recognizable songs bring, especially to those of us who would otherwise find ourselves sitting on the outside circle of the family orchestra.

Have you thought about orchestrating the sounds in your home? Stop and listen. What do you hear? Does it please you? Does it set you on edge? Could you add or subtract some notes to enhance your atmosphere?

I have found background music to be a pleasing greeting as guests arrive, though music can also be distracting if your friends feel they have to compete with it to converse. Sometimes the most accommodating background sound is silence, while other times music is a festive and hospitable addition.

Chimes on the porch can be a gentle touch; however, some are more like clanging cymbals that rankle the nervous system. But just as people see differently, we also hear differently. I stayed in a hotel recently where the housekeeper evidently thought I'd enjoy waking up at three in the morning to a hard-rock concert blaring from my radio. What may be a rip-snortin' clang to one may be an angelic choir to another. I have found that to be moderate in volume and style on the music dial is generally a good rule of thumb for guests. After everyone leaves, if you want to crank up your woofers and tweeters, have at it!

Speaking of tweeters, don't you just love the serenading songs of birds? In Michigan we are enchanted with the sound and sight of robins, our harbingers of spring. And with summer come troops of talented tweeters to our yard and gardens, adding visual joy and distinctive songs. From the cooing morning doves to the evening insistent whippoorwills and all the songsters in between (cardinals, bluebirds, finches), the outdoor concert drifts melodically into our home. Even the squawky blue jays' colorful rendition of "I did it my way" is appreciated in the mix. In the fall Michigan's sky fills with noisy, migrating Canadian geese. They honk as if to alert us to get out of town before the bitter winds blanket us in snow.

Snow was a way of life for my husband's family in the Upper Peninsula of Michigan.

The silent, accumulating snow caused noisy snowplows to generate a regular clamor. Because Les, his dad, and his brothers were lumberjacks by trade, they nightly heard the scrape and grind of the sharpening wheel preparing their axes for the following day. The two-hundred-pound, six-inch-wide wheel was hand cranked by the family and was used from spring straight through into winter.

I surveyed a few folks concerning house sounds that have remained with them from childhood. Some of the responses included yelling, bickering, and nagging. Yikes! That's not what I wanted to hear. But then, I guess they didn't either.

Come to think of it, much of the noise in our homes we create by the sounds from our own mouths. We are instructed to "make a joyful noise …" (Psalm 100:1a, KJV), which Les and I believe our mothers generally did. (Nah, they weren't perfect.) My mom filled our home with song as she worked around the house. That joyous offering convinced me she loved caring for us. And that thought added to my feelings of worth.

Les recollects the comforting sound of his mom's (Lena's) voice in the midst of a harsh environment with an abusive father. As if she carried a healing balm for bruised spirits, his mom poured out kindness to her children. Her gentle nature was a buffer during blustery family times.

My friend Marilyn remembers with fondness her mom's soft humming. Judy recalls the steady rhythm of the sewing machine filling their home. At that machine her mom faithfully designed their clothing and contributed to the family income.

Can you list five sounds that have affected your life? What sounds comfort and encourage the people surrounding you? What is the quality of your words? How will you be remembered by those you love most? Is your home filled with celebration or contention? What will you do today to help arrange for your family and friends to experience a sweet serenade?

Cherished Sounds

Footsteps of someone we love	Dinner Bell	Music
Laughter	Affirmation	Doorbell
Ice Cream Truck	Bread Machine	Purring
Splashing	Church Bells	Crickets
Yes	No	Maybe

"I love you, I love you, I love you!"

$\mathcal{S}$erenade P.S.

$\mathcal{M}$y parents were known by us children, for a happy sound they made— singing musical ditties. They would trill oldies like "Ka-Ka-Ka-Katie." "Katie" if you are uninformed, met her boyfriend when the moon shined over the cow shed at the kit-kit-kit-kitchen door. One of my favorites was "How Much Is That Doggie in the Window?" Not only did I like the melody, I also desperately wanted a puppy. But, alas, I was a second child, and my parents were all worn out on pets from their first child, my brother, Don. So my dog days didn't arrive until I was married and we had our own children.

Through our thirty-six years of marriage, Les and I have had a myriad of mutts— a frantic Russian wolfhound, a forceful standard poodle, a frenetic beagle … the list goes on. Some came and left within a short time. But two of them stayed and stayed and stayed. We liked that. Each added her own serenade of noises to our home. The click of paws, the whining, the panting, and the barking that announced company were all sweet sounds to us.

One dog who stayed put with us was a cockapoo named Tuesday who lived to be eleven. She was a sturdy dog for her breed and a steady producer of puppies, who were noise factories in their own right. Even though Tuesday was what you might call promiscuous, she was a faithful family dog.

When Tuesday passed away, I decided we must have another dog to keep Jason company. His only sibling, Marty, had joined the Air Force, and now Tuesday had left too, so I went puppy-shopping. When I saw this sweet little doggie in the window—the one with the waggily tail—I knew she was the one. I slipped the little shitzu into a basket, placed a bow around her neck, and presented her to a very happy recipient, Jason.

Pumpkin turned out to be an odd little character. For one thing, she thought she was a cat. She would crouch down and then, with hunched shoulders, stalk her food dish and pounce upon it as if it were a mouse. I told her repeatedly, "No, Pumpkin, you're a dog." Somehow her true identity eluded her for a long time. I thought perhaps she had been taken from her mom too soon and was suffering from separation anxiety. What she needed was a role model. But even my best attempts at imitating Lassie didn't seem to help. Besides, my knees were becoming calloused and the barking left my throat sore.

Pumpkin added an odd sound to our house that not every dog could contribute. She had a habit of murmuring. Folks often thought she was growling, when in fact she was talking to them and about them. This murmur became part of the symphony of our home. It's probably best we didn't know exactly what she was saying; we

just knew she had the gift of grumble. Pumpkin would have been a comfortable addition to the murmuring Israelites in the wilderness—as she was to the grumbling Clairmonts in the Midwest.

Pumpkin wasn't fond of anything smaller than she was. One day my nephew Steven brought over his new miniature dachshund. One glance from this baby wiener sent Pumpkin noiselessly plunging under the couch for refuge. Squeezing her chubby frame under our swayback couch was no easy achievement. I tried to coax Pumpkin out, but she refused my efforts with deep, guttural murmurs. It wasn't until the puppy left that Pumpkin crawled out, with spring prints pressed into her cowardly coat.

Predicting Pumpkin's behavior was impossible, for while she retreated at the sight of a puppy she was noisily willing to get right in the faces of the big guys. Our neighbors owned Maggie, a rambunctious Airedale who was always delighted to see Pumpkin when they were both let out to romp about their individual yards. The fence between them was good because our grumbler was a tad territorial. One day, Maggie's owner, Alicia, dropped by with her sanguine dog at her side. When I opened the door, Maggie inquisitively stuck her face in our house, probably looking for her (cough) friend Pumpkin. From who knows where, little Pumpkin—who actually snarled—leaped up and tried to remove Maggie's nose.

Pumpkin was unusual for her breed in that she was neither a yipper nor a nipper (with the two exceptions of Maggie and Nicholas). She was more a snorer and a

borer. Most of the time she was satisfied to take siestas, although she was definitely willing to work for food. I had taught her as a puppy to sit, lie down, roll over, speak, and dance. From that time on, when offered a treat, she would do all five tricks in quick succession to obtain a goodie. Then she'd nap … again. Her snore rumbling through the house like an off-key vacuum cleaner told us she was in La-La Land.

This zany little shitzu was very selective with people. She greeted everyone with sloppy enthusiasm but grew bored almost instantly. Her favorite long-term people were our children. So when Jason married Danya, Pumpkin moved into their home to live. For the past two and one-half years she has only paid visits to our abode, or we have visited her at their house.

In May of this year, Pumpkin, our tail-wagging doggie in the window, had to be put to sleep because of extreme health issues that could no longer be corrected. She would have been fourteen years old in September. She left behind a grateful fan club who will miss her funny clamberings, her dancing heart, and her constant stream of murmuring. Those sounds were for many years an important part of our family's serenade.

Each home's pet adds his or her personal touches of noise that tell us this is a place of warmth, comfort, and belonging. Creatures of varying sizes and personalities are welcomed into our homes and offered love, which they return in abundance—along with mischief and sometimes even murmurings.

$\mathscr{S}$weet Fragrances

$\mathscr{I}$ love to hear a grumbling bread machine working through its paces because I know the sound is the forerunner to an incredible aroma. Is there anything homier than the fragrance of baking bread? Hmm … coffee? Well, maybe for some. Coffee does have a way of filling up every corner and enticing even the caffeine reluctant. Or how about baking cookies or sizzling bacon? Oh, my, this is making me hungry not only for food but also for smells. Our sense of smell can be very satisfying, whether we are sniffing around the kitchen, a perfume counter, or a garden.

I remember being on a strict food program some years ago (it's obviously not been recent), in which, when I needed a chocolate fix, I'd hang out at the Godiva counter and just breathe in deeply. This was my version of chocolate by osmosis, and it actually helped. Sometimes just getting over the hump of chocolate deprivation can assist one in making it another … well, say, twenty minutes.

A new-old fad of aromatherapy is receiving a lot of press these days. Its main claim is that we are affected by smells, and if we can learn how a smell affects us then we can either avoid it or inhale it for positive results.

Positive effects come my way when my husband bastes hamburgers in his super-duper secret sauce as he grills on the deck. That he is cooking instead of me already emits the sweet smell of success. When he adds to the dinner an iron skillet of fried potatoes smothered in onions and garlic (be still, my sniffing nose) with roasted corn on the cob … well, I'm one happy camper.

But food isn't the only bouquet that delights our sense of smell. Ask my rose-sniffing daughter-in-law or me, her lilac-whiffing mother-in-law. Danya and I both love flowers, especially if they surround us in our homes. I remember reading once that Jacqueline Onassis was sunning on her terrace when her husband showered her in rose petals via an airplane. Now that's more than a fragrant memory, that's down-right romantic.

Isn't it amazing that scents, like sounds, hold memories? It seems they store up inside like a soda, and, when you pop the cap, the fizz and smell release the memory. Les says wood stoves pop his cap.

Les grew up in a home heated by a wood furnace, and his mom cooked on a wood-fueled stove. So he and his five siblings were involved in cutting, splitting, stacking, carrying, and fueling. Since the winters in the Upper Peninsula were harsh, fires were a constant way of life. No wonder the smell of burning wood still floods him with childhood feelings.

Les also salivates at even the thought of his mom's Finnish meat pies, called pasties. The meat pies had alternating layers of potatoes, onions, rutabagas, carrots, and hamburger or venison. All of the ingredients were encased in a crust, and each pasty weighed about one and one-half pounds to satisfy her lumberjack family. She usually prepared thirty pasties at a time, which meant the baking went on for hours, allowing the smell to saturate their home and their memories.

One scented memory that has remained sweet for me is my mom's favorite cream sachet. I loved how, at the close of a day, when she tucked me in bed and kissed me good night, the smell of her sachet would linger in the air. I found that comforting and reassuring. And I remember slipping into her supply so I, too, could smell pretty.

Another fragrant freeze frame of my mom was of her hanging clothes on the line to absorb the outdoor freshness. Her little four-foot, ten-inch frame, clothed in a tidy shirtwaist dress, stretched to reach the clotheslines. Wooden clothespins filled her apron pockets while a few were perched between her teeth. She deftly emptied the contents of her woven baskets onto the lines with the skill that comes only from experience. When the clotheslines were full, the sheets waved in the perfumed breeze, promising her family a night of summer dreams.

I didn't realize when I was young how valiantly my mom cared for our home and family. I rarely praised her efforts—that is, until I had a home of my own and realized what it takes to keep a house organized, lovely, and fragrant.

"Fragrant" was part of Mom's home strategy. For instance, she was always airing the house. Doors and windows were opened, creating a glorious cross breeze. Then she would scrub and shine every room until the house glowed and smelled of furniture polish, floor wax, cleanser, and room deodorizer (the kind in a bottle with a big fat wick attached to the cap). How invigorating to walk through such sparkling, aromatic rooms. To this day I love to walk in someone's home after they have cleaned and aired to catch that delicious scent of cleanliness.

I have learned a few tricks through the years to help with freshness. I, like my mom, keep a box of baking soda in the refrigerator to absorb strong odors. I occasionally squeeze the juice from a lemon (or diluted Tang) into my garbage disposal to keep it from being offensive. I have also been known to put a touch of vanilla on my stove burner to send forth a delicious aroma. And, of course, I recirculate the air in my home regularly.

Yet the sweetest bouquet I can release in my home is Christ's presence. He generously offers to peruse the rooms of my interior and carefully inspect the corners. Christ alone knows what I need that will freshen my attitudes, air my stale thoughts, and cleanse my soiled heart. When I emit his character (through kindness, industriousness, and sweetness), the fragrance is undeniable and irresistible, for he is the Lily of the Valley and the Rose of Sharon.

Cherished Fragrances

Seasonings

Oranges

Citrus blossoms

Pine trees

Hot chocolate

Leather

Rain

Aftershave

Honeysuckle

Cedar

Mulled cider

Roasting turkey

Finishing Touches

My mom was the queen of finishing touches. She just knew how to take the extra steps to transform ordinary into exceptional. Whether it was a meal she had prepared, a room she was decorating, a party she was throwing, a class she was teaching, or an outfit she was sporting, Mom excelled in dynamics. Her finishing efforts made her crystal gleam, her throw rugs fluff, her pillows poof, her flowers arrange, her mirrors sparkle, her cupboards attractive, her food memorable, and her company cheer.

My mom could even balance her checkbook and transact a business deal with the same grace she used to press every wrinkle from her family's wardrobe. Am I like my mom? Well, yes and no. I am not numerical; I'm more into verbiage. Numbers don't compute for me unless they are on a telephone pad. (Recently, I saw a lady in a T-shirt that read, "Help! I'm on the telephone, and I can't stop talking!") Along with mastering numbers, my mom always seemed to have more control over her stuff than I do. Mine tends to spew out of closets, spill out of drawers, and dribble out from under the beds, which, when unattended, can defeat any finishing touches.

I guess the part of my mom I share is our delight in the spiffy touches. After I've packed down my drawers' spillage, kicked the dribble back under the bed, and corralled the spew (eew!), then I'm ready, willing, and eager to add a touch-up here and there. The only time finishing touches aren't fun is when I've procrastinated, and I'm running at breakneck speed to try to accomplish my tasks. Then my whole household tends to pay the price for my frayed nerves. Ask them. No, wait … just trust me, okay?

A finishing touch will normally cost you more time and creative thought than money. Even your time can be minimized once you get the gist of it. The essential pallet for a lovely home is cleanliness and neatness. These "nesses" are extremely important as a decorating foundation because it's really difficult to notice and appreciate, say, a vase of daisies in the midst of chaos. What could have been a highlight in a room becomes lost in the jumble if you have no order to your existence. I'm not talking perfection but a sane system for allowing you to control your home and not let your home rule you.

For me, as a young agoraphobic (physically and emotionally housebound) wife and mom, disorder abounded in my sphere. When I began to deal with my depression and my anxiety (inch by inch), I also began to establish new disciplines (inch by inch), which aided me in eventually bringing order (inch by inch) to my home. In other words, my outer disarray was a sign of my inner turmoil, and both needed to be addressed.

I'm grateful that, when life began to come together for me, I was able to draw from what I had learned and observed via my mom on how to cherish my home and those who entered therein. In the beginning, her standards were too all-encompassing for me, and I had to learn realistic standards for my home and myself. Then I had to incorporate consistent habits to help me maintain my home's basic appearance before I took on finishing touches.

Gradually, I entered into the joy of arranging bouquets, napkins, pictures, furniture, and such. I found it thrilling to look at a tidy room and ask myself what I could do to make the surroundings more hospitable, more attractive, more colorful, and more interesting. Then I would proceed. Sometimes a table just needed a bowl of fruit. I would select the right size and color bowl and arrange the fruit, making sure to polish the apples, rinse the grapes, and remove all the stickers. Or maybe I would note it was time to rotate lamps and pictures to give a fresh ambiance to the place.

I've learned that less sometimes is more. This is not an easy lesson for my exaggeration-prone personality type. For instance, a single rose can be as beautiful as a full bouquet. And in certain settings it makes the greater impact. Also, a centerpiece can be a perfect finishing touch, but beware: There is no end to how much you can invest in one. You can simply fill a basket with pine cones from your yard, add a bow and—voila!—a lovely centerpiece graces your table. (If you don't have time to let your cones air-dry, put them in the oven on a low setting long enough to remove the threat of little critters joining your party.) Through the winter I have a stack of picturesque birch logs next to my fireplace. The holly bush outside our door offers me festive sprigs that I tuck in the center of bows, on packages, in arrangements, on door handles, and even on my stack of logs.

As a young wife, I hesitated to try to spiff up our house because we were on such a restricted budget. Then I realized how many things I could do without busting our piggy bank. But does a tidy house, a bowl of fruit, a basket, a pine cone, a log, a sprig constitute a dynamic environment? Alone they would be overlooked, but together they make an undeniable statement about how you creatively cherish your home, family, and others. Seldom will a person fix up that which she doesn't care about.

Speaking of fixing up, I just came in from outside where, for a brain break, I deadheaded some petunias and pansies. While perusing the garden, I was smitten once again with the finishing touches of our Creator. He could have just given us petunias and pansies, and I would have been forever fascinated with them (one that trumpets, one that smiles). But he added brilliant poppies, stunning roses, charming geraniums, and breathtaking bougainvillea. And this just for starters. He also sent the aerobatic, iridescent, comedic hummingbird to dart and flash about the petals, sipping sweet nectar in colorful twitches, not to mention the exquisitely patterned butterflies and the chubby, fuzzy-jacketed bumblebees. He carpeted the earth in emerald and released refreshing rains. Then, for a finale, he set the rainbows in the heavens and spilled them down onto the earth. Wow! Some folks just know how to add finishing touches.

I recently visited a restaurant-inn outside of Washington, D.C. Our group of fourteen (thirteen women and one nervous man) was impressed with how every square inch of the inn had been tended to. We felt as if these folks cared about whether we returned by the very way they prepared for us and cared for us. Fragrant bouquets were everywhere, even in the restroom stalls. The service was impeccable, and the food was as attractive to look at as it was delicious to eat. After a spectacular dessert, as a closing statement, we were presented with tiny straw baskets chucked full of finger-tip delicacies to take home. We all oohed and aahed … all the way home (a two-hour drive).

I find it personally satisfying to establish ambiance, create interest, and add a final touch in my home. But I am reminded that the most important and impressive imprint we leave is our genuine interest in and love for others. One of the sweetest recollections for our guests to take away is that we cared enough to share our time and to truly listen to them. Never underestimate your touch in another life … we never know when it may be a final one.

Final Touches

A thank-you poem	A compliment	A hug
A scrapbook	A bubble bath	A cup of tea
A turned-down bed	A bedside book	A sunset
A ribbon	Dessert	Our prayers

Eventide

"Good night" is a term of endearment. It whispers, "Rest well"; it speaks peace to the soul; and it conveys, God willing, that we will meet again in a new day.

I love the privacy of the evening hours in which one can cuddle up on the sofa with loved ones and hear the details of their day. Or snuggle with a marvelous book in preparation for renewing sleep. Or steep in a bubble bath until the day slips away.

I also love a clear evening sky strewn with a gazillion stars and perhaps just a slice of new moon. But enough light is shed to be mirrored in still ponds where crickets sing and frogs grumble and where winds whisper secrets to pondering owls.

But night also brings doubts. We tend to feel unsure about what we can't see (that's why faith is so challenging for us), so we cover our windows and lock our doors. Actually, I enjoy that ritual, for these purposed steps bring safety, protection, privacy, and closure to the daylight hours. And while we fasten the night out, we secure people in, which draws us closer. As we turn from the outside world, we are exclusively with each other.

Les and I share the journey of pulling down shades and locking up doors. We only have two doors to lock, but we cover twenty windows. Two small leaded-glass windows in our living room, which are high, do not require coverings. I'm pleased because these *au naturel* panes safely allow night's mystery to seep in. The moonlight is pretty through the paned glass, though I must say the light is even lovelier in the day because the leaded glass fractures the sunlight into prisms that scatter, like confetti, across the floor.

Many evenings we wait until late to close the wood verticals that cover our French doors in the kitchen. We enjoy watching the moon ignite the snow, causing crystal sparkles to dance across our backyard. And sometimes old man moon reveals a scampering rabbit or a marauding raccoon. But mostly he just runs a narrow path of light to our door like an invitation we are tempted to accept.

Evening at our home is a time for winding down as our energy fizzles out, a time when our beds coax us toward a dreamy respite. I have to climb up a step stool to reach our towering bed. Then I scootch under the comforter and bury my face in the down pillow. Oh, blessed relief. The weight is off my feet (whew), and I can finally exhale (ahhh) and allow the gift of sleep to embrace me (zzz).

Have you ever awakened uncertain of where you are? My speaking schedule keeps me on the road regularly, and nothing is more disorienting than to be startled awake and then confused as to my whereabouts. I guess that's why I so appreciate waking up in our home with those whom I cherish most. These are the ones with whom I have made lasting memories through uproarious laughter and heart-wrenching tears.

These are the ones who have dined at my table, shared books I love, and sipped from my saucerful of secrets. This is the place and these are the people whom I cherish most and who most cherish me. Yes, to be at home is so settling; it is reassuring; it is my favorite place to be … day or evening.

> "They [the Levites] were also to stand every morning to thank and praise the Lord. They were to do the same in the evening."
>
> 1 CHRONICLES 23:30

Dear Lord Jesus,

We stand and deliberately praise you, you who are worthy of praise! Thank you for night's sleep and dawn's strength. Thank you for paths of light in the dead of night and the invitation to follow you in trust. Thank you for family comforts and for the promise that we can rest in you. *Amen.*

Our Shepherd never slumbers
so sleep, sheep.